MCA-III Prep
Grade 3 Mathematics
Second Edition

by Jonathan D. Kantrowitz

Edited by Christina M. Roush and Philip W. Sedelnik

Item Code RAS3119 • Copyright © 2012 Queue, Inc.

Queue, Inc. • 80 Hathaway Drive • Stratford, CT 06615
(800) 232-2224 • Fax: (800) 775-2729 • www.qworkbooks.com

Table of Contents

Minnesota Academic Standards for Mathematics—Grade 3	Pages/ Problem #'s
Number and Operation	**Pages 1–80**
3.1.1 Compare and represent whole numbers up to 10,000, with an emphasis on place value.	Pages 1–27
1. Read, write and represent whole numbers up to 10,000. Representations may include numerals, expressions with operations, words, pictures, number lines, and manipulatives such as bundles of sticks and base 10 blocks.	Problems 1–41
2. Use place value to describe whole numbers between 1,000 and 10,000 in terms of groups of thousands, hundreds, tens and ones.	Problems 42–68
3. Find 1,000 more or 1,000 less than any given four-digit number. Find 100 more or 100 less than a given four-digit number.	Problems 69–76
4. Round numbers to the nearest 1,000, 100 and 10. Round up and round down to estimate sums and differences.	Problems 77–106
5. Compare and order whole numbers up to 10,000.	Problems 107–154
3.1.2 Add and subtract multi-digit whole numbers; represent multiplication and division in various ways; solve real-world and mathematical problems using arithmetic.	Pages 28–69
1. Add and subtract multi-digit numbers, using efficient and generalizable procedures based on knowledge of place value, including standard algorithms.	Problems 155–270
2. Use addition and subtraction to solve real-world and mathematical problems involving whole numbers. Assess the reasonableness of results based on the context. Use various strategies, including the use of a calculator and the relationship between addition and subtraction, to check for accuracy.	Problems 271–311

3. Represent multiplication facts by using a variety of approaches, such as repeated addition, equal-sized groups, arrays, area models, equal jumps on a number line and skip counting. Represent division facts by using a variety of approaches, such as repeated subtraction, equal sharing and forming equal groups. Recognize the relationship between multiplication and division.	Problems 312–325
4. Solve real-world and mathematical problems involving multiplication and division, including both "how many in each group" and "how many groups" division problems.	Problems 326–371
5. Use strategies and algorithms based on knowledge of place value and properties of addition and multiplication to multiply a two- or three-digit number by a one-digit number. Strategies may include mental strategies, partial products, the standard algorithm, and the commutative, associative, and distributive properties.	Problems 372–377
3.1.3 Understand meanings and uses of fractions in real-world and mathematical situations.	Pages 70–80
1. Read and write fractions with words and symbols. Recognize that fractions can be used to represent parts of a whole, parts of a set, points on a number line, or distances on a number line.	Problems 378–402
2. Understand that the size of a fractional part is relative to the size of the whole.	Problems 403–408
3. Order and compare unit fractions and fractions with like denominators by using models and an understanding of the concept of numerator and denominator.	Problems 409–416

Algebra	Pages 81–87
3.2.1 Use single-operation input-output rules to represent patterns and relationships and to solve real-world and mathematical problems.	Pages 81–82
1. Create, describe, and apply single-operation input-output rules involving addition, subtraction and multiplication to solve problems in various contexts.	Problems 417–424
3.2.2 Use number sentences involving multiplication and division basic facts and unknowns to represent and solve real-world and mathematical problems; create real-world situations corresponding to number sentences.	Pages 83–87
1. Understand how to interpret number sentences involving multiplication and division basic facts and unknowns. Create real-world situations to represent number sentences.	Problems 425–454
2. Use multiplication and division basic facts to represent a given problem situation using a number sentence. Use number sense and multiplication and division basic facts to find values for the unknowns that make the number sentences true.	Problems 455–462
Geometry and Measurement	Pages 88–113
3.3.1 Use geometric attributes to describe and create shapes in various contexts.	Pages 88–91
1. Identify parallel and perpendicular lines in various contexts, and use them to describe and create geometric shapes, such as right triangles, rectangles, parallelograms and trapezoids.	Problems 463–469
2. Sketch polygons with a given number of sides or vertices (corners), such as pentagons, hexagons and octagons.	Problems 470–473

3.3.2 Understand perimeter as a measurable attribute of real-world and mathematical objects. Use various tools to measure perimeter.	Pages 92–97
1. Use half units when measuring distances.	Problems 474–482
2. Find the perimeter of a polygon by adding the lengths of the sides.	Problems 483–498
3. Measure distances around objects.	Problems 499–500
3.3.3 Use time, money and temperature to solve real-world and mathematical problems.	Pages 98–113
1. Tell time to the minute, using digital and analog clocks. Determine elapsed time to the minute.	Problems 501–524
2. Know relationships among units of time.	Problems 525–542
3. Make change up to one dollar in several different ways, including with as few coins as possible.	Problems 543–556
4. Use an analog thermometer to determine temperature to the nearest degree in Fahrenheit and Celsius.	Problems 557–565
Data Analysis	**Pages 114–149**
3.4.1 Collect, organize, display, and interpret data. Use labels and a variety of scales and units in displays.	Pages 114–149
1. Collect, display and interpret data using frequency tables, bar graphs, picture graphs and number line plots having a variety of scales. Use appropriate titles, labels and units.	Problems 566–629
About The Practice Tests	**Page 151**
Pretest	T1
Posttest	T31

Express each of the following numbers in words.

1. 68

2. 91

3. 117

4. 284

5. 395

Express each of the following numbers in words.

6.   523

7.   604

8.   728

9.   862

10.   939

2

Express each of the following numbers in standard form.

11.   forty-nine

12.   seventy-seven

13.   one hundred fifty-six

14.   two hundred eighty-three

15.   four hundred seventeen

3

Express each of the following numbers in standard form.

16.   seven hundred twelve

17.   eight hundred thirty-four

18.   nine hundred fourteen

19.   nine hundred twenty-seven

20.   nine hundred ninety-two

Express each of the following numbers in words.

21.   928   24.   462

22.   364   25.   525

23.   623   26.   876

Express each of the following numbers in words.

27. 734

30. 829

28. 1,000

31. 620

29. 106

32. 742

1 △ = 100   1 ◯ = 10   1 ☐ = 1

Write the number 351 in two different ways using the symbols shown above.

33. First Way:

34. Second Way:

35.

If one ⬜ equals 100, one ▯ equals 10, and one ☐ equals 1, which of the following diagrams shows 283?

a.

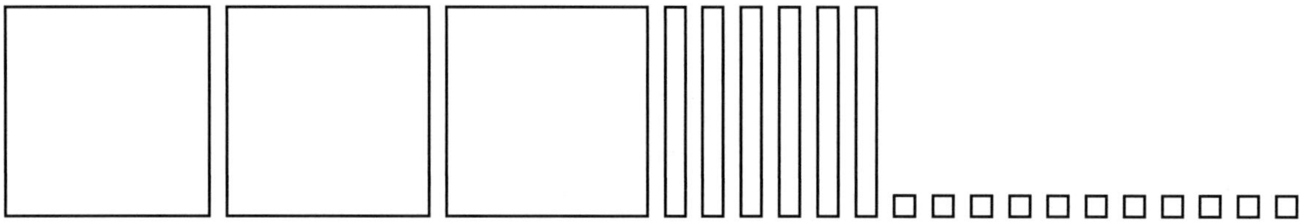

b.

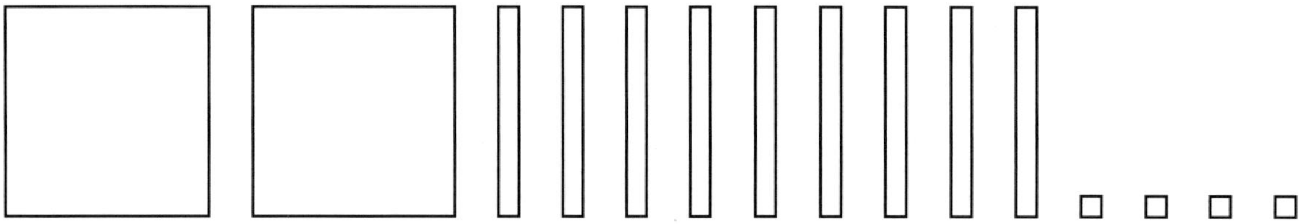

c.

d.

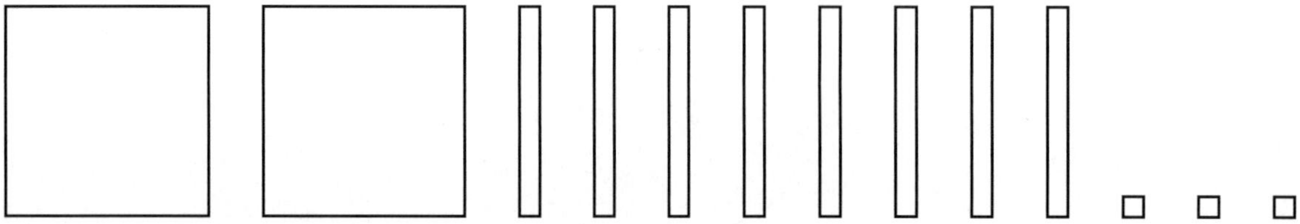

Match the following numbers to the correct base ten block representation.

36. 57 _____

37. 36 _____

38. 28 _____

39. 34 _____

40. 62 _____

41. 21 _____

A

B

C

D

E

F

42. Which of the following means the same as three thousands and 14 hundreds?

    a. 4,400
    b. 4,140
    c. 3,014
    d. 4,014

43. Which of the following means the same as ten hundreds?

    a. 10
    b. 900
    c. 1,000
    d. 100

44. Which of the following means the same as four thousands and seven tens?

    a. 4,700
    b. 4,770
    c. 4,007
    d. 4,070

45. Which of the following means the same as 17 hundreds and five tens?

    a. 5,070
    b. 1,750
    c. 1,570
    d. 1,705

46. Which of the following numerals means the same as one thousand, two hundreds, nine tens, and four ones?

    a. 1,500
    b. 1,213
    c. 1,294
    d. 2,094

47. The number 5,643 can be grouped as

    a. five thousands, six hundreds, five tens, and thirteen ones.
    b. four thousands, five hundreds, four tens, and three ones.
    c. five thousands, six hundreds, four tens, and three ones.
    d. five thousands, four hundreds, six tens, and three ones.

48. The number 2,275 can be grouped as

    a. two thousands, one hundred, seven tens, and five ones.
    b. two thousands, two hundreds, seven tens, and five ones.
    c. two thousands, three hundreds, three tens, and five ones.
    d. one thousand, two hundreds, seven tens, and fifteen ones.

10

49. How would 3,365 be written in expanded form?

    a. 3 x 1,000 +
        3 x 100 +
        6 x 100 +
        5 x 10

    b. 3 x 1,000 +
        3 x 100 +
        6 x 10 +
        5 x 1

    c. 3 x 1,000 +
        3 x 100 +
        6 x 10 +
        9 x 1

    d. 3 x 1,000 +
        3 x 1,000 +
        6 x 100 +
        5 x 10

52. How would 6,242 be written in expanded form?

    a. 6 x 1,000 +
        2 x 1,000 +
        4 x 100 +
        4 x 10

    b. 6 x 10,000 +
        2 x 10,000 +
        4 x 1,000 +
        2 x 100

    c. 6 x 10,000 +
        2 x 10,000 +
        4 x 1,000 +
        4 x 10

    d. 6 x 1,000 +
        2 x 100 +
        4 x 10 +
        2 x 1

Write the following numbers in expanded notation.

50. 5,118

51. 2,649

Write the following numbers in expanded notation.

53. 3,227

54. 1,863

Write each of the following numbers in expanded notation.

55. 4,327 =

58. 1,842 =

56. 2,642 =

59. 3,958 =

57. 7,775 =

60. 8,464 =

12

61. How would 3,439 be written in expanded form?

    a. 3 x 1,000 +
         4 x 100 +
         3 x 100 +
         9 x 10

    b. 3 x 100 +
         4 x 10 +
         3 x 10 +
         9 x 10

    c. 3 x 1,000 +
         4 x 100 +
         3 x 10 +
         9 x 1

    d. 3 x 1,000 +
         4 x 1,000 +
         3 x 100 +
         9 x 10

63. How would 9,474 be written in expanded form?

    a. 9 x 1,000 +
         4 x 1,000 +
         7 x 100 +
         4 x 10

    b. 9 x 10,000 +
         4 x 10,000 +
         7 x 1,000 +
         4 x 100

    c. 9 x 10,000 +
         4 x 10,000 +
         7 x 1,000 +
         4 x 10

    d. 9 x 1,000 +
         4 x 100 +
         7 x 10 +
         4 x 1

62. Janet saved 1,056 pennies. Which of the following would be another way to show 1,056?

    a. 1 thousand + 5 tens + 6 ones
    b. 1 thousand + 13 tens + 6 ones
    c. 1 thousand +14 tens + 6 ones
    d. 1 thousand + 13 tens + 16 ones

64. Fred collected 297 bugs. Which of the following is another way to show 297?

    a. 2 hundreds +4 tens + 7 ones
    b. 2 hundreds + 9 tens + 7 tens
    c. 2 hundreds + 9 tens + 7 ones
    d. 2 hundreds + 14 tens + 7 ones

65. Which of the following numerals means the same as four thousands, two hundreds, nine tens, and four ones?

    a. 215
    b. 4,213
    c. 4,294
    d. 2,094

66. The number 3,275 can be grouped as

    a. three thousands, one hundred, seven tens, and five ones.
    b. three thousands, two hundreds, seven tens, and five ones.
    c. three thousands, three hundreds, three tens, and five ones.
    d. two thousands, two hundreds, seven tens, and fifteen ones.

$$1,000 + 800 + 90 + 5$$

67. How would the above number be written in standard form?

    a. 1,598
    b. 1,958
    c. 1,985
    d. 1,895

68. The number 2,643 can be grouped as

    a. one thousand, six hundreds, five tens, and thirteen ones.
    b. one thousand, five hundreds, four tens, and three ones.
    c. two thousands, six hundreds, four tens, and three ones.
    d. two thousands, four hundreds, six tens, and three ones.

69. 3,672 + 1,000 =

a. 4,672
b. 3,772
c. 4,783
d. 2,672

73. 6,297 + 1,000 =

a. 7,297
b. 7,318
c. 6,397
d. 6,307

70. 5,981 - 1,000 =

a. 5,881
b. 4,870
c. 4,971
d. 4,981

74. 8,538 - 1,000 =

a. 9,538
b. 8,538
c. 7,538
d. 8,438

71. 7,589 + 100 =

a. 8,589
b. 7,689
c. 7,579
d. 6,589

75. 9,312 + 100 =

a. 10,312
b. 9,322
c. 9,412
d. 9,212

72. 3,356 - 100 =

a. 4,556
b. 3,356
c. 3,256
d. 3,346

76. 2,857 - 100 =

a. 1,857
b. 1,957
c. 2,847
d. 2,757

Round each of the following numbers to the nearest ten.

77. 79

78. 276

79. 11

80. 74

81. 96

Round each of the following numbers to the nearest hundred.

82. 822

83. 271

84. 740

Round each of the following numbers to the nearest thousand.

85. 2,857

86. 3,475

87. One morning a baker made 328 muffins. Round this number to the nearest ten.

88. It is 71 miles from Boston, MA, to Concord, NH. Round this number to the nearest ten.

    a. 60
    b. 65
    c. 70
    d. 80

89. Elm Farm grew 624 pumpkins last year. Round this number to the nearest hundred.

90. Sally was in the the Empire State Building in New York City. The building is 1,454 feet tall. Round this number to the nearest hundred.

91. Leon has 882 coins in his coin jar. Round this number to the nearest ten.

17

92. Smith needs to add 72 and 61. Which of the following would be BEST for Smith to ESTIMATE the sum of these two numbers?

    a. 80 + 60
    b. 90 + 70
    c. 70 + 60
    d. 70 + 70

94. Dave wants to add 26, 49, and 78. Which of the following would give Dave the BEST ESTIMATE?

    a. 20 + 40 + 70
    b. 20 + 50 + 60
    c. 30 + 50 + 70
    d. 30 + 50 + 80

93. Farmer Mike's last count of animals showed he owned 28 sheep, 67 cows, and 23 pigs. Write a number sentence that would be BEST for Mike to use to ESTIMATE of the total number of animals he owns.

95. Ben wants to add 49, 40, and 68. Which of the following would give Ben the BEST ESTIMATE?

    a. 50 + 40 + 70
    b. 60 + 50 + 60
    c. 50 + 50 + 70
    d. 70 + 70 + 40

96. Two weeks ago Kristina read 19 pages in her history book. Last week she read 24 pages, and this week she read 21 pages. ABOUT how many pages has she read in all?

    a. 70
    b. 50
    c. 40
    d. 60

97. Paula sold 28 tickets to the school play. Richard sold 71 tickets. Which is the BEST ESTIMATE of how many more tickets Richard sold than Paula?

    a. 100
    b. 50
    c. 40
    d. 30

98. Mrs. Hill and Mr. Smith have jars of candy in their classrooms. There are 710 pieces in Mrs. Hill's jar and 191 pieces in Mr. Smith's jar. Which is the BEST ESTIMATE of the total number of pieces of candy in both jars?

    a. 600
    b. 700
    c. 800
    d. 900

99. Felix wants to add 78 and 37. Which of the following would be BEST for Felix to use to ESTIMATE this sum?

    a. 80 + 30
    b. 90 + 20
    c. 80 + 40
    d. 90 + 40

100. Kim wants to subtract 332 from 788. Which of the following would be BEST for Kim to use to ESTIMATE this difference?

    a. 780 - 330
    b. 800 - 330
    c. 790 - 330
    d. 800 - 320

101. Harmon wants to estimate the difference between 579 miles and 916 miles. Which of the following would be BEST for Harmon to use to make that estimate?

    a. 900 - 600
    b. 900 - 500
    c. 900 - 400
    d. 800 - 600

19

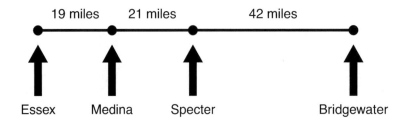

19 miles   21 miles   42 miles

Essex   Medina   Specter   Bridgewater

102. Which of the following would BEST be used to ESTIMATE the total distance from Essex to Bridgewater?

    a. 10 + 10 + 40
    b. 10 + 10 + 50
    c. 10 + 20 + 50
    d. 20 + 20 + 40

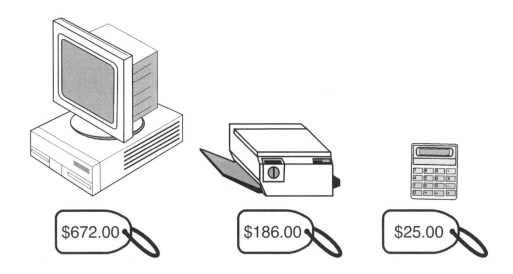

$672.00 $186.00 $25.00

103. Which of the following would BEST be used to ESTIMATE the amount needed to buy all three items?

    a. $670 + $160 + $40
    b. $660 + $170 + $30
    c. $650 + $180 + $20
    d. $670 + $190 + $25

104. Teddy was given the numbers 87, 148, and 319 to add. He said that the sum of these three numbers was about 560. Is this a reasonable estimate of the sum of these three numbers? Explain your answer.

106. Jeff was given the numbers 868 and 242. He said the difference between these two numbers was about 500. Is this a reasonable estimate of the difference between these two numbers? Explain your answer.

105. Which of the following number sentences shows the BEST ESTIMATE of the distance, in miles, from Medina to Specter?

    a. 30 + 30 + 40
    b. 10 + 20 + 40
    c. 20 + 30 + 40
    d. 10 + 20 + 30

21

In each of the following problems, circle the LARGER number.

107.

115   375

108.

281   161

109.

96   104

110.

952   925

111.

819   809

112.

80   167

113.

563   436

114.

312   213

115.

461   507

116.

293   452

22

In each of the following problems, circle the SMALLER number.

117.

    61   68

122.

    138   135

118.

    318   327

123.

    244   258

119.

    900   910

124.

    538   568

120.

    483   471

125.

    991   929

121.

    779   782

126.

    539   693

23

Complete the following number sentences by writing **>**, **<**, or **=** in the circles below.

127. 569 $\bigcirc$ 203

128. 35 $\bigcirc$ 23

129. 356 $\bigcirc$ 785

130. 3,597 $\bigcirc$ 203

131. 4,856 $\bigcirc$ 3,238

132. 3,594 $\bigcirc$ 1,756

133. 4,527 $\bigcirc$ 475

134. 7,854 $\bigcirc$ 7,854

Arrange the following numbers from LARGEST to SMALLEST:

		867		935

a.   933

b.   431

c.   673

d.   480

e.   127

f.   550

141. Which of the following numbers is
     NOT between 867 and 935?

     a. 901
     b. 872
     c. 884
     d. 945

135. _____

136. _____

137. _____

142. Which group of numbers is in
     order from LEAST to GREATEST?

     a. 227   226   209   212
     b. 209   212   226   227
     c. 212   226   209   227
     d. 227   209   226   212

138. _____

139. _____

143. Which group of numbers is in
     order from GREATEST to LEAST?

     a. 347   346   343   341
     b. 349   342   346   346
     c. 342   346   349   346
     d. 347   349   346   343

140. _____

25

School Name	Number of Third Graders
Central	102
Hill	87
Garza	110
Wilson	93

144. The number of third graders at each elementary school in Caprock City is shown on the above chart. Which of the following lists the schools in order from LEAST to GREATEST number of third graders?

    a. Hill, Central, Wilson, Garza
    b. Central, Garza, Hill, Wilson
    c. Hill, Wilson, Central, Garza
    d. Garza, Central, Wilson, Hill

145. Caprock City is going to open a new elementary school which will have 95 third graders. Which school(s) in Caprock City will have MORE third graders than this school?

In each of the following problems, circle the larger number.

146.   356   785

147.   569   203

148.   894   756

149.   527   550

150.   624   642

151.   91   100

152.   854   258

Student	Magazines Sold
Ernie	143
Norma	125
D.J.	138
David	146
Stephanie	130

153. The above table shows the amount of magazines sold by five students in a fundraiser. Which student sold the MOST magazines?

154. Which group of numbers is in order from LEAST to GREATEST?

a. 227   326   309   512
b. 309   512   326   527
c. 512   326   309   527
d. 227   309   326   512

27

Add the following numbers.

155.
$$
\begin{array}{r}
17 \\
+\,36 \\
\hline
\end{array}
$$

159.
$$
\begin{array}{r}
45 \\
+\,22 \\
\hline
\end{array}
$$

156.
$$
\begin{array}{r}
28 \\
+\,59 \\
\hline
\end{array}
$$

160.
$$
\begin{array}{r}
81 \\
+\,15 \\
\hline
\end{array}
$$

157.
$$
\begin{array}{r}
48 \\
+\,33 \\
\hline
\end{array}
$$

161.
$$
\begin{array}{r}
63 \\
+\,26 \\
\hline
\end{array}
$$

158.
$$
\begin{array}{r}
19 \\
+\,68 \\
\hline
\end{array}
$$

162.
$$
\begin{array}{r}
38 \\
+\,49 \\
\hline
\end{array}
$$

Add the following numbers.

163.   62
     + 59

167.   74
     + 78

164.   33
     + 86

168.   90
     + 25

165.   48
     + 97

169.   86
     + 99

166.   41
     + 53

170.   94
     + 57

Add the following numbers.

171. $\begin{array}{r} 44 \\ + 64 \\ \hline \end{array}$

172. $\begin{array}{r} 98 \\ + 11 \\ \hline \end{array}$

173. $\begin{array}{r} 71 \\ + 36 \\ \hline \end{array}$

174. $\begin{array}{r} 33 \\ + 85 \\ \hline \end{array}$

175. $\begin{array}{r} 52 \\ + 26 \\ \hline \end{array}$

176. $\begin{array}{r} 34 \\ + 53 \\ \hline \end{array}$

177. $\begin{array}{r} 25 \\ + 61 \\ \hline \end{array}$

178. $\begin{array}{r} 43 \\ + 24 \\ \hline \end{array}$

30

Add the following numbers.

179.
$$104$$
$$+\ 125$$

183.
$$491$$
$$+\ 203$$

180.
$$217$$
$$+\ 311$$

184.
$$522$$
$$+\ 817$$

181.
$$153$$
$$+\ 205$$

185.
$$680$$
$$+\ 320$$

182.
$$456$$
$$+\ 801$$

186.
$$593$$
$$+\ 299$$

31

Add the following numbers.

187. $\begin{array}{r} 171 \\ + 364 \\ \hline \end{array}$

191. $\begin{array}{r} 456 \\ + 226 \\ \hline \end{array}$

188. $\begin{array}{r} 288 \\ + 593 \\ \hline \end{array}$

192. $\begin{array}{r} 810 \\ + 159 \\ \hline \end{array}$

189. $\begin{array}{r} 484 \\ + 336 \\ \hline \end{array}$

193. $\begin{array}{r} 631 \\ + 266 \\ \hline \end{array}$

190. $\begin{array}{r} 195 \\ + 687 \\ \hline \end{array}$

194. $\begin{array}{r} 386 \\ + 497 \\ \hline \end{array}$

32

In each of the following problems, find the sum.

195.
$$172$$
$$+113$$

198.
$$372$$
$$+402$$

196.
$$247$$
$$+150$$

199.
$$417$$
$$+381$$

197.
$$302$$
$$+291$$

200.
$$564$$
$$+335$$

33

In each of the following problems, find the sum.

201.
$$\begin{array}{r} 270 \\ +208 \\ \hline \end{array}$$

204.
$$\begin{array}{r} 518 \\ +361 \\ \hline \end{array}$$

202.
$$\begin{array}{r} 341 \\ +337 \\ \hline \end{array}$$

205.
$$\begin{array}{r} 650 \\ +246 \\ \hline \end{array}$$

203.
$$\begin{array}{r} 472 \\ +427 \\ \hline \end{array}$$

206.
$$\begin{array}{r} 853 \\ +126 \\ \hline \end{array}$$

34

Add the following numbers shown below.

207. $\begin{array}{r} 4,178 \\ +\ 4,326 \\ \hline \end{array}$

211. $\begin{array}{r} 5,353 \\ +\ 7,914 \\ \hline \end{array}$

208. $\begin{array}{r} 6,534 \\ +\ 3,038 \\ \hline \end{array}$

212. $\begin{array}{r} 8,837 \\ +\ 9,963 \\ \hline \end{array}$

209. $\begin{array}{r} 7,612 \\ +\ 2,237 \\ \hline \end{array}$

213. $\begin{array}{r} 7,622 \\ +\ 4,264 \\ \hline \end{array}$

210. $\begin{array}{r} 7,959 \\ +\ 8,551 \\ \hline \end{array}$

214. $\begin{array}{r} 5,073 \\ +\ 9,327 \\ \hline \end{array}$

Add the following numbers shown below.

215. $\begin{array}{r} 6,264 \\ +\ 2,492 \\ \hline \end{array}$

219. $\begin{array}{r} 9,532 \\ +\ 1,465 \\ \hline \end{array}$

216. $\begin{array}{r} 3,464 \\ +\ 1,487 \\ \hline \end{array}$

220. $\begin{array}{r} 6,348 \\ +\ 9,954 \\ \hline \end{array}$

217. $\begin{array}{r} 8,126 \\ +\ 2,235 \\ \hline \end{array}$

221. $\begin{array}{r} 5,286 \\ +\ 4,481 \\ \hline \end{array}$

218. $\begin{array}{r} 3,268 \\ +\ 8,265 \\ \hline \end{array}$

222. $\begin{array}{r} 5,465 \\ +\ 1,167 \\ \hline \end{array}$

Subtract the following numbers.

223.   59
      - 37
      ―――

227.   93
      - 49
      ―――

224.   88
      - 71
      ―――

228.   81
      - 47
      ―――

225.   94
      - 53
      ―――

229.   72
      - 65
      ―――

226.   47
      - 40
      ―――

230.   99
      - 89
      ―――

37

Subtract the following numbers.

231.
$$\begin{array}{r} 139 \\ -64 \\ \hline \end{array}$$

235.
$$\begin{array}{r} 322 \\ -51 \\ \hline \end{array}$$

232.
$$\begin{array}{r} 177 \\ -82 \\ \hline \end{array}$$

236.
$$\begin{array}{r} 246 \\ -168 \\ \hline \end{array}$$

233.
$$\begin{array}{r} 103 \\ -91 \\ \hline \end{array}$$

237.
$$\begin{array}{r} 507 \\ -416 \\ \hline \end{array}$$

234.
$$\begin{array}{r} 215 \\ -73 \\ \hline \end{array}$$

238.
$$\begin{array}{r} 739 \\ -364 \\ \hline \end{array}$$

Subtract the following numbers.

239.
$$\begin{array}{r} 821 \\ -\ 354 \\ \hline \end{array}$$

243.
$$\begin{array}{r} 544 \\ -\ 367 \\ \hline \end{array}$$

240.
$$\begin{array}{r} 633 \\ -\ 282 \\ \hline \end{array}$$

244.
$$\begin{array}{r} 426 \\ -\ 317 \\ \hline \end{array}$$

241.
$$\begin{array}{r} 541 \\ -\ 176 \\ \hline \end{array}$$

245.
$$\begin{array}{r} 675 \\ -\ 578 \\ \hline \end{array}$$

242.
$$\begin{array}{r} 293 \\ -\ 88 \\ \hline \end{array}$$

246.
$$\begin{array}{r} 908 \\ -\ 809 \\ \hline \end{array}$$

Subtract the following numbers.

247.
$$
\begin{array}{r}
590 \\
-\ 372 \\
\hline
\end{array}
$$

251.
$$
\begin{array}{r}
933 \\
-\ 498 \\
\hline
\end{array}
$$

248.
$$
\begin{array}{r}
888 \\
-\ 711 \\
\hline
\end{array}
$$

252.
$$
\begin{array}{r}
811 \\
-\ 473 \\
\hline
\end{array}
$$

249.
$$
\begin{array}{r}
946 \\
-\ 532 \\
\hline
\end{array}
$$

253.
$$
\begin{array}{r}
722 \\
-\ 657 \\
\hline
\end{array}
$$

250.
$$
\begin{array}{r}
470 \\
-\ 400 \\
\hline
\end{array}
$$

254.
$$
\begin{array}{r}
999 \\
-\ 891 \\
\hline
\end{array}
$$

40

Subtract the following numbers shown below.

255.
$$\begin{array}{r} 5,687 \\ -\ 3,471 \\ \hline \end{array}$$

259.
$$\begin{array}{r} 5,756 \\ -\ 2,454 \\ \hline \end{array}$$

256.
$$\begin{array}{r} 7,918 \\ -\ 6,705 \\ \hline \end{array}$$

260.
$$\begin{array}{r} 6,847 \\ -\ 3,626 \\ \hline \end{array}$$

257.
$$\begin{array}{r} 8,439 \\ -\ 8,216 \\ \hline \end{array}$$

261.
$$\begin{array}{r} 4,998 \\ -\ 3,234 \\ \hline \end{array}$$

258.
$$\begin{array}{r} 1,994 \\ -\ 1,072 \\ \hline \end{array}$$

262.
$$\begin{array}{r} 2,869 \\ -\ 1,753 \\ \hline \end{array}$$

Subtract the following numbers shown below.

263.
$$\begin{array}{r} 4{,}037 \\ -\ 1{,}471 \\ \hline \end{array}$$

267.
$$\begin{array}{r} 6{,}006 \\ -\ 2{,}454 \\ \hline \end{array}$$

264.
$$\begin{array}{r} 7{,}918 \\ -\ 3{,}705 \\ \hline \end{array}$$

268.
$$\begin{array}{r} 6{,}847 \\ -\ 3{,}026 \\ \hline \end{array}$$

265.
$$\begin{array}{r} 9{,}059 \\ -\ 8{,}216 \\ \hline \end{array}$$

269.
$$\begin{array}{r} 7{,}998 \\ -\ 3{,}004 \\ \hline \end{array}$$

266.
$$\begin{array}{r} 4{,}124 \\ -\ 2{,}072 \\ \hline \end{array}$$

270.
$$\begin{array}{r} 6{,}309 \\ -\ 1{,}753 \\ \hline \end{array}$$

271. There are six birds in a tree. Two birds fly away. How many birds are left?

272. There are 312 boys and 482 girls in a school. How many children are there altogether?

273. Ray had five marbles. He lost four of them. How many marbles did he have left?

274. Dick had seven marbles at home, 19 in a bag, and ten in his pocket. How many marbles did he have altogether?

275. Five children were playing. Two children went home. How many children were left to play?

276. Joe had 29 papers to sell. After he sold 15 of them, how many did he have left?

277. In which of the following pairs of numbers is the first number 10 less than the second number?

    a. 79 and 179
    b. 289 and 1,289
    c. 99 and 109
    d. 839 and 840

278. Michael wants to buy two new programs for his computer. They cost $29.95 each. If his mother gives him $40.00, how much more does he need to buy the programs?

279. Mr. Dobbs drove six hundred thirty-five miles in two days. If he drove three hundred sixteen miles the first day, how many miles did he drive the second day?

    a. three hundred ninety-one miles
    b. three hundred nineteen miles
    c. two hundred ninety-seven miles
    d. four hundred nine miles

280. Lorraine has 16 cookies. She gave five cookies to Cindy and six cookies to Dana. Which number sentence shows how many cookies Lorraine now has?

    a. 16 x 11 =
    b. 16 + 5 + 6 =
    c. 16 + 5 - 6 =
    d. 16 - 5 - 6 =

281. Carla was born in 1970. When she was twenty years old, she started college. Seven years later, she started her own business. Which number sentence shows the year Carla started her own business?

    a. 1970 - 20 + 7
    b. 1970 + 20 - 7
    c. 1970 - 20 - 7
    d. 1970 + 20 + 7

282. There are 51 cards on a table. There are different ways to group the 51 cards into three piles. Which of the following is NOT a way to group the cards?

    a. 21 + 20 + 11
    b. 20 + 20 + 11
    c. 15 + 15 + 21
    d. 17 + 17 + 17

283. Chris is 156 centimeters tall and Josie is 120 centimeters tall. Which number sentence could be used to find how many centimeters taller Chris is than Josie?

   a. 156 - 120 =
   b. 120 ÷ 56 =
   c. 56 + 120 =
   d. 156 x 120 =

285. One morning, a baker made 328 loaves of bread. He sold 315 loaves of bread during the day. Which of the following could be used to determine the number of loaves he has left?

   a. 328 x 315
   b. 328 + 315
   c. 328 ÷ 315
   d. 328 - 315

284. Jack weighs 88 pounds. Which of the following could be used to find how many more pounds Jack must gain before he weighs 100 pounds?

   a. 100 - 88
   b. 100 + 88
   c. 88 x 88
   d. 100 x 100

286. Jeff was playing pinball on his computer. In his first turn, Jeff scored 435 points. On his second turn, Jeff scored 755 points. Which of the following could be used to find out how many more points Jeff scored on his second turn than on his first turn?

   a. 755 - 435
   b. 755 + 435
   c. 435 x 2
   d. 755 ÷ 2

287. Dina wants to buy a new computer. She saw one that cost $875.00 and another one that cost $790.00. How much more does the first computer cost than the second computer?

    a. $85.00
    b. $105.00
    c. $75.00
    d. $115.00

288. Sonia bought a shirt that cost $13.00, including tax. Sonia paid for the shirt with a twenty-dollar bill. How much change should she receive?

    a. $7.00
    b. $13.00
    c. $3.00
    d. $10.00

289. Jim sold 78 newspapers one day. The next day he sold 38. In these two days, how many newspapers did he sell?

290. A train traveled 391 miles on Monday and 507 miles on Tuesday. Altogether, how many miles did the train travel in these two days?

    a. 814
    b. 898
    c. 906
    d. 794

291. Mona read 12 books in the first grade, 19 books in the second grade, and 28 books in the third grade. How many books has Mona read?

    a. 68
    b. 59
    c. 39
    d. 44

292. Judy has 325 baseball cards, Tony has 175, and Nancy has 110. Altogether, how many baseball cards do the three children have?

    a 500
    b. 435
    c. 610
    d. 600

Month	Number of Books Read
September	750
October	1,347
November	1,431
December	687

293. Mrs. Larson, the principal, agreed to have a party if the students reached their goal of reading 5,000 books. Using the information in the chart shown above, write an expression to determine how many books the students have read so far.

294. Alberta had 52 marbles. She was given 47 more marbles. Which of the following shows how many total marbles Alberta now has?

   a. 52 - 47 = 5
   b. 52 + 47 = 99
   c. 99 + 52 = 151
   d. 99 + 47 = 146

295. There are 47 people waiting in line. If Kerri is the fifth person in line, how many people are behind her in this line?

296. Gus read three books in August. The first book had 80 pages. The second had 75 pages, and the third had 68 pages. Two of the books were fiction and one was non-fiction. How many pages did Gus read in August?

297. Irma and Juan are both in high school. Irma has completed 12 book reports. Juan has completed 20 book reports. Juan has gone to three chess club meetings. How many book reports have Juan and Irma completed altogether?

298. Jill has 28 CDs, and John has 45 CDs. Jill went to 10 concerts in the last year and John has been to three. How many CDs do Jill and John have altogether?

299. Kyle likes to learn new words from the dictionary. He has looked up 65 new words this year. His friend Leon has looked up 40 new words this year. They both have seen 10 of their new words in a video game. How many words have Leon and Kyle looked up in total this year?

300. Dan had $0.64. How much money did he have after he bought a pencil for $0.29?

    a. $0.45
    b. $0.44
    c. $0.35
    d. $0.34

301. Last year, 47 boys and 41 girls attended Wilson School. Altogether, how many children attended Wilson School last year?

302. Mr. Soto has $50.00. In a store he saw a shirt for $26.00 and a belt for $18.00. If he buys the belt, which shows how to find how much money he will have left?

    a. 50 + 18
    b. 50 + 26 - 18
    c. 50 - 18
    d. 50 - 26 - 18

303. Duane had $0.45, then picked up $0.38 he found on the ground. How much money does Duane now have?

304. Raphael went to the board and worked the problem 31 - 9. He got an answer of 22. Which of the following could Raphael use to check his answer for this problem?

    a. 22 + 9
    b. 22 - 9
    c. 31 + 9
    d. 31 + 22

Jane and her Dad drove 68 miles from their home to Brooklawn. From there they drove 163 miles to Candlewood Lake. How much farther was it from Brooklawn to Candlewood Lake than from their home to Brooklawn?

305. The number sentence for this problem is

a. 68 - 163.
b. 163 - 68.
c. 213 - 68.
d. 231 - 68.

306. The answer is _____ miles.

a. 96
b. 89
c. 95
d. 88

307. Kate has 57 more beanbag animals than Brad. Brad has 42 beanbag animals. How many beanbag animals does Kate have?

a. 98
b. 86
c. 109
d. 99

308. Which is a correct way to solve question 307?

a. 57 + 42 =
b. 57 - 42 =
c. 57 ÷ 42 =
d. 57 x 42 =

Nadyezhda Tkachenko of the U.S.S.R. set the Olympic record for the women's pentathlon in 1980 by scoring 5,083 points. Sigrun Siegl of East Germany won the same event in 1976, scoring 4,745 points. How much higher was Tkachenko's score than Siegl's score?

309. The best way to solve this problem is to

a. add, then subtract.
b. add.
c. subtract.
d. subtract, then multiply.

310. How can this problem be expressed?

a. 5,083 - 4,745
b. 5,083 + 4,745
c. 5,083 x 4,745
d. 1,980 - 1,976

311. Tkachenko's score was _____ points higher than Siegl's score.

a. 328
b. 346
c. 325
d. 338

312. Last Saturday, Brian went jogging in the park. Including Brian, there were only three joggers. This Saturday, there are five times as many joggers in the park than there were last Saturday. Which of the following diagrams best shows the number of joggers in the park this Saturday?

a.

c.

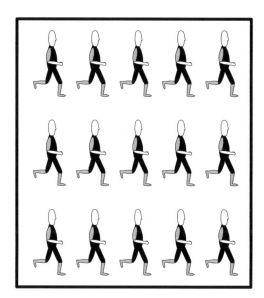

b.

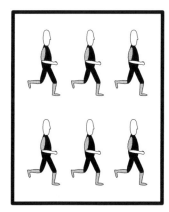

d.

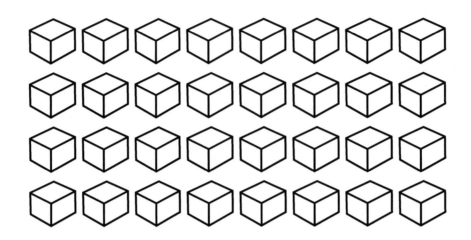

313. Which of the following number sentences BEST reflects the arrangement of blocks shown in the above diagram?

   a. 8 x 3 =
   b. 8 x 4 =
   c. 7 x 5 =
   d. 7 x 6 =

1	🌹 🌹 🌹 🌹 🌹 🌹 🌹 🌹 🌹 🌹 🌹
2	
3	
4	
5	

314. Jamie is planting a flower bed like the one shown above. If Jamie plants 11 roses in each of the five rows of her flower bed, which of the following can be used to find out how many roses she will plant altogether?

   a. 11 x 11 =
   b. 11 x 5 =
   c. 5 x 5 =
   d. 5 + 11 =

315. Which of the following diagrams shows a 5 x 4 array?

a.

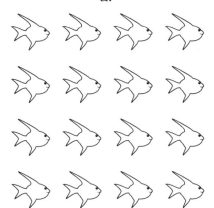

c.

b.

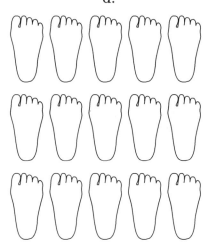

d.

316. Which of the following diagrams best shows four times three?

a.

b.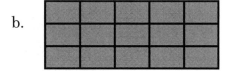

c.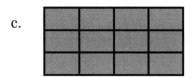

d.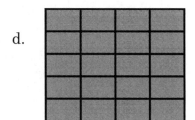

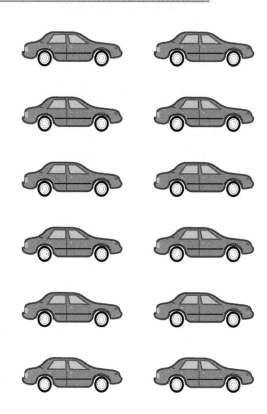

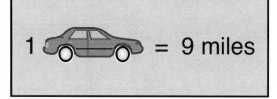

1 🚗 = 9 miles

317. How many total miles does the above diagram show?

a. 90 miles
b. 108 miles
c. 81 miles
d. 124 miles

54

318. Which of the following number sentences can be used to find the number of stars in the above array?

    a. 4 x 6 =
    b. 3 x 7 =
    c. 5 x 8 =
    d. 2 x 10 =

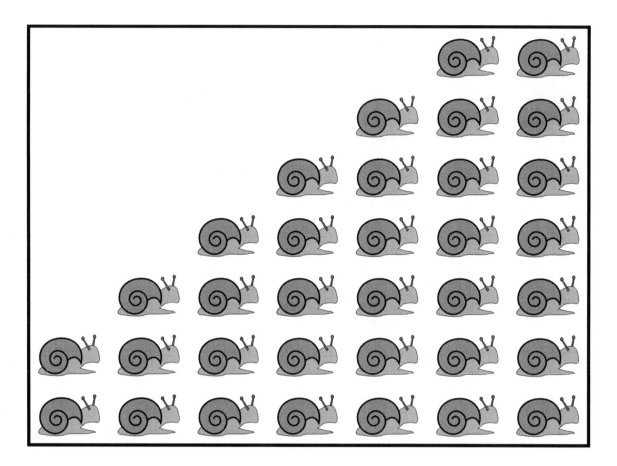

1 🐌 = 15 snails

319. Which of the following is the BEST ESTIMATE of the total number of snails shown in the above diagram?

    a. 200 snails
    b. 300 snails
    c. 400 snails
    d. 500 snails

320. Lisa, Donna, Zak, and Adriana each have five balloons. Which picture below shows how many balloons they have altogether?

a.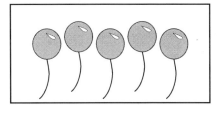

b.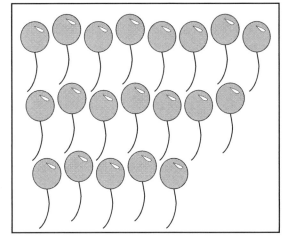

c.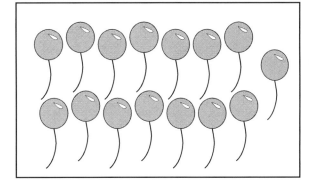

d.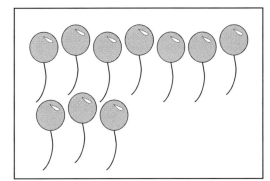

321. The flowers shown above can be used to show that

    a. 24 x 3 = 36.
    b. 24 ÷ 3 = 8.
    c. 24 + 3 = 27.
    d. 24 ÷ 3 = 6.

322. The people shown above can be used to show that

    a. 6 x 2 = 12.
    b. 3 x 3 = 9.
    c. 6 + 3 = 9.
    d. 6 ÷ 3 = 2.

323. Which of the following could be shown by the bulbs in the diagram above?

    a. 8 x 3 = 24
    b. 24 ÷ 3 = 8
    c. 18 ÷ 3 = 6
    d. 24 ÷ 8 = 3

324. Which of the following could be shown by the geese in the diagram above?

    a. 8 x 3 = 24
    b. 24 ÷ 3 = 8
    c. 18 ÷ 3 = 6
    d. 21 ÷ 3 = 7

59

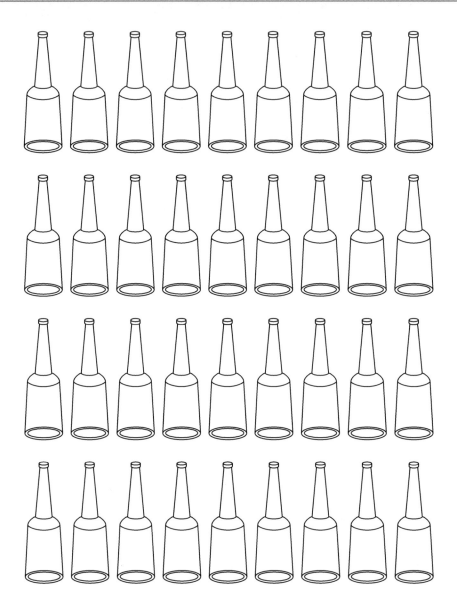

325. Which of the following could be shown by the bottles in the diagram above?

    a. 40 ÷ 10 = 4

    b. 36 ÷ 9 = 4

    c. 36 ÷ 10 = 4

    d. 10 x 4 = 40

If 656 ÷ 4 = 164 then,

326. If you divided 656 marbles into 4 equal groups, each group would contain

    a. 16 marbles.
    b. 14 marbles.
    c. 164 marbles.
    d. 4 marbles.

327. If you took 164 marbles away from the original 656 marbles 4 times, you would have how many marbles left?

    a. 164
    b. 656
    c. 16
    d. 0

328. If you took 4 marbles at a time away from the original 656, you would have to do it _____ times before all the marbles were gone.

    a. 164
    b. 656
    c. 4
    d. 0

329. If 68 x 76 = 5,168, then 5,168 ÷ 76 =

    a. 67.
    b. 69.
    c. 76.
    d. 68.

330. If 12,963 ÷ 3 = 4,321, then 4,321 x 3 =

    a. 963
    b. 12,963
    c. 8,642
    d. 4,321

331. If 737 x 564 = 415,668, then 415,668 ÷ 737 =

    a. 564
    b. 654
    c. 456
    d. 546

332. If 3,942 ÷ 304 = 13, then 3.942 ÷ 13 =

    a. 13 x 304
    b. 304 ÷ 13
    c. 304
    d. 13

333. Fifteen people, including Kitty, were coming to dinner. Kitty would be in charge of setting the table. Each person was to get two spoons. How many spoons did Kitty need?

    a. 30
    b. 36
    c. 18
    d. 24

334. The 80 third-grade students in Martin Luther King School are going on an all-day field trip. The cost for each student is $8.00. What is the total cost for all 80 students?

    a. $360.00
    b. $1,600.00
    c. $640.00
    d. $720.00

335. Jason filled his baseball card book by putting nine cards on each of the 52 pages. How many baseball cards does he have in his book?

336. Ray bought eight notebooks. Each notebook contained 75 sheets of paper. How many sheets of paper did Ray buy?

    a. 570
    b. 600
    c. 625
    d. 700

337. Mary bought 13 boxes of cream puffs. There were four cream puffs in each box. How many cream puffs did she buy?

    a. 36
    b. 45
    c. 52
    d. 34

338. Dwayne has 5 boxes of toy cars. Each box has 12 cars in it. How many toy cars does Dwayne have in all?

    a. 50 cars
    b. 60 cars
    c. 75 cars
    d. 115 cars

339. Dwayne has 5 boxes of toy cars. Each box has 12 cars in it. Which of the following can be used to find out how many toy cars Dwayne has in all?

    a. 12 + 5
    b. 12 x 5
    c. 12 ÷ 5
    d. 12 - 7

340. The local supermarket sells eight cases of tomato sauce every week. There are twelve cans of tomato sauce in a case. Which of the following can be used to find out how many cans of tomato sauce are sold in one week?

    a. 7 x 8
    b. 8 x 8
    c. 12 x 8
    d. 12 x 7

341. Sasha's class held a spelling bee. There were 32 students in the class. Each team had six students. One student was a word reader and one was a spelling checker. Which of the following can be used to find out how many teams were in the spelling bee?

    a. (32 + 1 + 1) x 6
    b. 32 ÷ (6 + 1 + 1)
    c. (32 - 1 - 1) ÷ (6 - 1)
    d. (32 - 1 - 1) ÷ 6

If you learn two new spelling words each day, how long will it take you to learn 80 new words?

342. Which of the following would be a correct way to solve the above problem?

    a. 80 ÷ 2 =
    b. 80 + 2 =
    c. 80 - 2 =
    d. 80 x 2 =

If one quart of ice cream will serve eight people, how many people will five quarts serve?

343. Which of the following would be a correct way to solve the above problem?

    a. 5 x 1 =
    b. 5 x 8 =
    c. 8 + 5 =
    d. 8 + 1 =

---

344. Ben has three letters in his first name. Elaine has two times as many letters in her first name. Which of the following could be used to find out how many letters are in Elaine's first name?

   a. 2 x 2
   b. 2 x 3
   c. 2 x 4
   d. 3 x 4

345. Candace goes to the gym three times a week. Which of the following could be used to find out how many times Candace goes to the gym in eight weeks?

   a. 3 x 6
   b. 3 x 7
   c. 3 x 8
   d. 3 x 9

346. A computer repair store had eleven customers on Monday. On Tuesday, the store had three times as many customers. Which of the following could be used to find out how many customers the store had on Tuesday?

   a. 11 x 3
   b. 11 x 4
   c. 11 x 5
   d. 11 x 6

347. Jason bought four cans of tomatoes at the supermarket each week for four weeks. Which of the following could be used to find out the total number of cans of tomatoes that Jason bought?

   a. 4 x 2
   b. 4 x 3
   c. 4 x 4
   d. 4 x 6

348. Justin drinks six glasses of water a day. Which of the following could be used to find out how many glasses of water Justin drinks in seven days?

   a. 5 x 6
   b. 6 x 7
   c. 6 x 8
   d. 8 x 7

349. Nina has four balloons. Her sister has nine times as many balloons. Which of the following could be used to find out how many balloons Nina's sister has?

   a. 4 x 6
   b. 4 x 7
   c. 4 x 8
   d. 4 x 9

64

350. Eight people were coming to dinner. Sam was setting the table. She gave each person 2 spoons. How many spoons did she need?

    a. 16
    b. 14
    c. 8
    d. 12

351. Tom earns $5 a week. How many weeks must he work to earn a new bicycle which costs $45?

    a. 7
    b. 8
    c. 9
    d. 10

352. A school buys 500 cartons of milk in 5 days. How many cartons of milk does the school buy for 1 day?

    a. 75
    b. 105
    c. 250
    d. 100

353. One quart of ice cream will serve 8 people. How many people will 5 quarts serve?

    a. 36
    b. 40
    c. 26
    d. 42

354. The third grade orders 8 cartons of milk each day. How many cartons do they use in 5 days?

    a. 36
    b. 32
    c. 42
    d. 40

355. How many 3-cent stamps can you buy for 36 cents?

    a. 12
    b. 15
    c. 9
    d. 10

65

356. Last Saturday three friends went to a movie. Rachel had $20.00 to pay for all of the tickets. Each ticket cost $4.00. Which method could be used to find the total cost of the tickets?

    a. Subtract 3 from 20.
    b. Add 3 and 4.
    c. Multiply 3 by 4.
    d. Divide 20 by 4.

357. Jack bought 5 packages of flower seeds. Each package had 5 seeds in it. How many flower pots does Jack need to buy if he wants to put one seed in each pot?

    a. 26
    b. 15
    c. 25
    d. 30

358. Kenny bought eight packs of hockey cards. Twelve cards are in each pack, and each pack costs $1.37, including sales tax. Which of the following methods could be used to find the total cost of the hockey cards that Kenny bought?

    a. Multiply 8 times 12.
    b. Multiply 8 times 12; then add $1.37.
    c. Multiply 8 times $1.37.
    d. Multiply 8 times 12 times $1.37.

359. Troy filled his stamp book by putting 36 stamps on each of its eight pages. How many stamps does Troy have in his book?

    a. 288
    b. 396
    c. 324
    d. 412

360. Wilson School had a party. Each child in Grade 3 brought in 5 cupcakes. There were 39 children in Grade 3. How many cupcakes did they bring?

    a. 156
    b. 172
    c. 205
    d. 195

361. Steve, Dan, Sarah and Holly all go to the movies together. Their tickets cost $32 total. Write an equation to find out how much each of their tickets cost, then solve the equation.

362. Laura had 20 nickels. She divided them into 4 equal piles. How many nickels were in each pile?

    a. 4
    b. 5
    c. 10
    d. 16

363. There are 17 tables in the school library. How many chairs will be needed for a meeting if 6 students sit at each table?

    a. 102
    b. 68
    c. 62
    d. 27

364. The El Rancho Diner buys 60 cartons of eggs each week. Each carton has 12 eggs. What is the total number of eggs the diner buys each week?

    a. 5
    b. 72
    c. 180
    d. 720

365. Billy is making wind chimes for his teachers. He has 15 bells, and he will use 5 bells for each wind chime. How many wind chimes will Billy make?

    a. 3
    b. 5
    c. 10
    d. 20

366. Mr. Méndez is buying hamburger buns for 28 hamburgers. Since hamburger buns come in packages of 6, how many packages of buns should Mr. Méndez buy?

    a. 3
    b. 5
    c. 10
    d. 15

367. An activity requires students to be in groups of four. There are twenty-eight students in Ms. Henderson's class. How many groups will there be?

    a. 6
    b. 7
    c. 24
    d. 31

368. If you learn 2 new spelling words each day, how long will it take you to learn 100 new words?

    a. 26 days
    b. 33 days
    c. 50 days
    d. 60 days

369. Four boys were playing with Fidel. Fidel's mother gave him 25 cookies to share. How many cookies did each boy get?

    a. 4
    b. 5
    c. 2
    d. 3

370. Tom gets 8 cents a box for picking cherries. How many boxes must he pick to earn 64 cents?

    a. 7
    b. 8
    c. 6
    d. 9

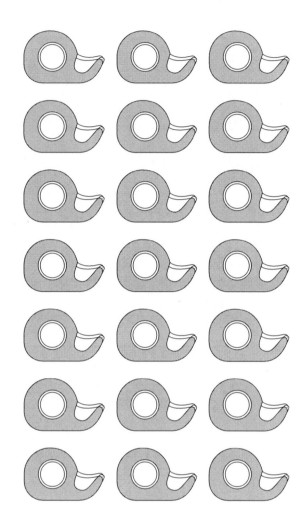

371. Which of the following could be used to find out the total number of rolls of tape shown in the above diagram?

    a. 8 x 2
    b. 7 x 3
    c. 7 x 4
    d. 6 x 4

372. 4 x 32 =

    a. 4 x 30 + 80
    b. 4 x 30 + 8
    c. 11 x 2 + 8
    d. 12 + 80

373. 5 x 12 =

    a. 5 x 10 + 5 x 2
    b. 5 x 20 + 5 x 1
    c. 5 x 10 + 5 x 20
    d. 50 x 10 + 5 x 2

374. 3 x 96 =

    a. 3 x 6 + 3 x 9
    b. 3 x 60 + 3 x 90
    c. 3 x 90 + 3 x 6
    d. 3 x 90 + 3 x 60

375. 6 x 73 =

    a. 7 x 6 + 30 x 6
    b. 70 x 6 + 3 x 6
    c. 7 x 60 + 3 x 60
    d. 70 x 60 + 30 x 60

376. 2 x 342 =

    a. 68 + 4
    b. 680 + 4
    c. 2 x 34 + 2 x 20
    d. 68 + 84

377. 9 x 123 =

    a. 9 x 120 + 30
    b. 9 x 12 + 30
    c. 9 x 12 + 27
    d. 9 x 120 + 27

Match each of the numbers expressed in words with its corresponding fraction.

378. one-half   _____   A $\dfrac{1}{5}$

379. one-fourth   _____   B $\dfrac{1}{2}$

380. one-fifth   _____   C $\dfrac{1}{8}$

381. one-sixth   _____   D $\dfrac{1}{10}$

382. one-eighth   _____   E $\dfrac{1}{6}$

383. one-tenth   _____   F $\dfrac{1}{4}$

Match each of the numbers expressed in words with its corresponding fraction.

384. three-fourths   _____   A $\dfrac{4}{5}$

385. five-eighths   _____   B $\dfrac{7}{10}$

386. two-thirds   _____   C $\dfrac{2}{3}$

387. four-fifths   _____   D $\dfrac{3}{4}$

388. seven-tenths   _____   E $\dfrac{5}{8}$

389. five-sixths   _____   F $\dfrac{5}{6}$

Match each of the fractions shown below with its corresponding picture.

390. $\dfrac{5}{8}$ _____   A

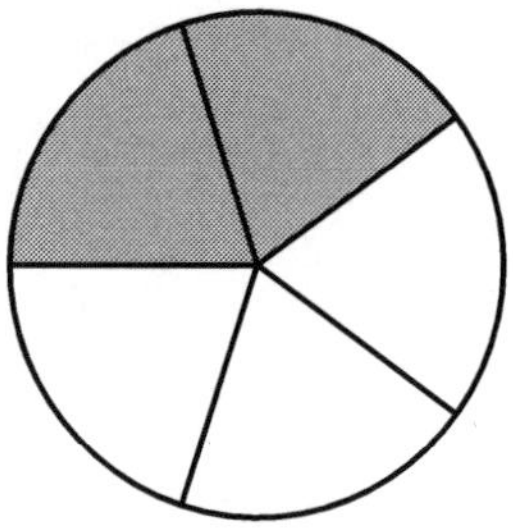

391. $\dfrac{2}{3}$ _____   B

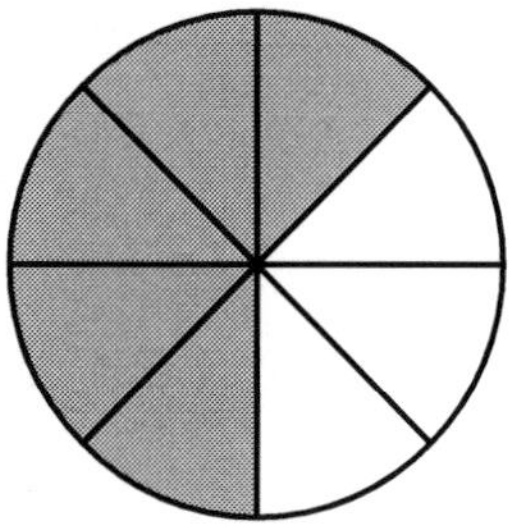

392. $\dfrac{3}{4}$ _____   C

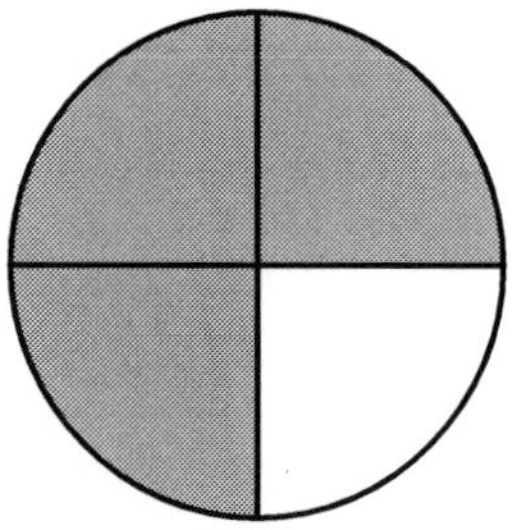

393. $\dfrac{1}{6}$ _____   D

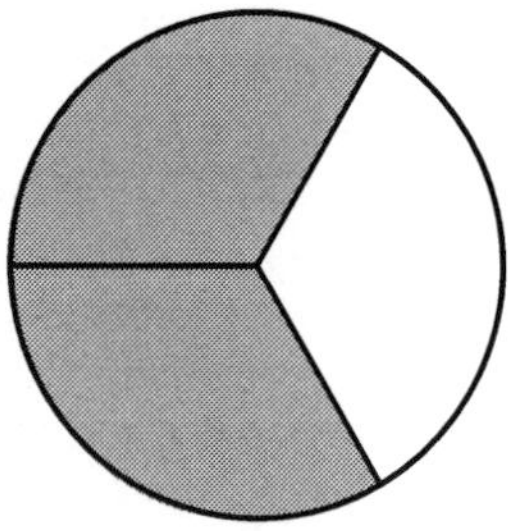

394. $\dfrac{2}{5}$ _____   E

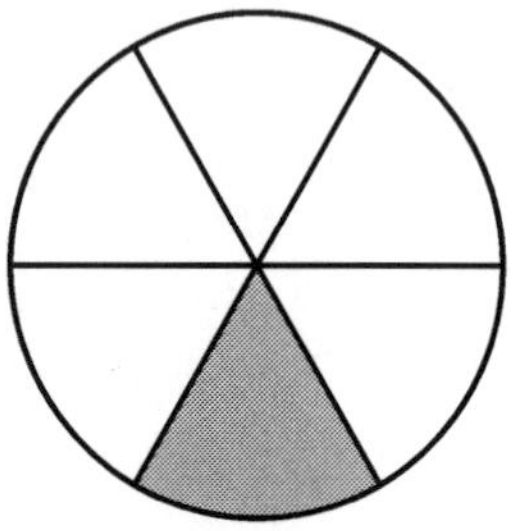

72

Match each of the fractions shown below with its corresponding picture.

395. $\dfrac{1}{3}$ _____

396. $\dfrac{5}{6}$ _____

397. $\dfrac{4}{5}$ _____

398. $\dfrac{3}{8}$ _____

399. $\dfrac{7}{10}$ _____

A

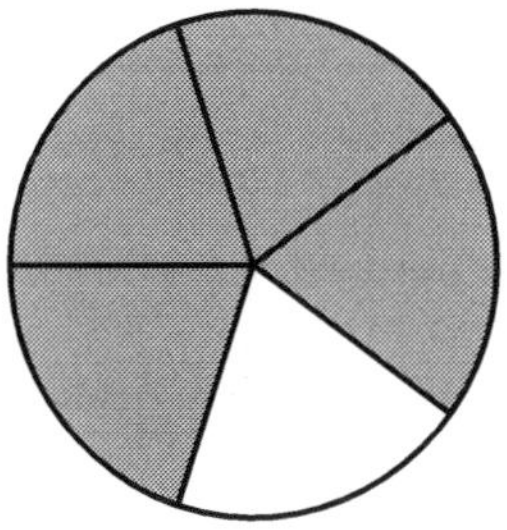

B

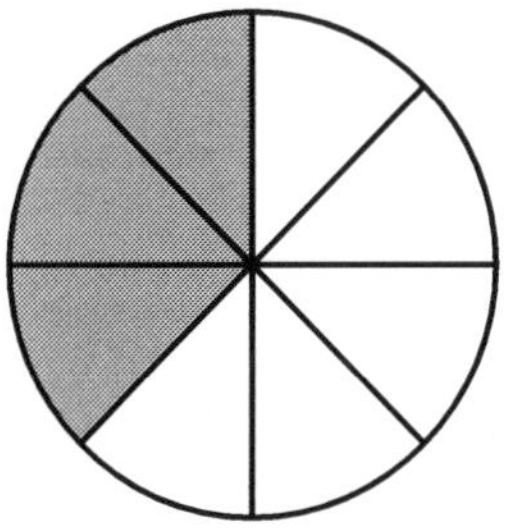

C

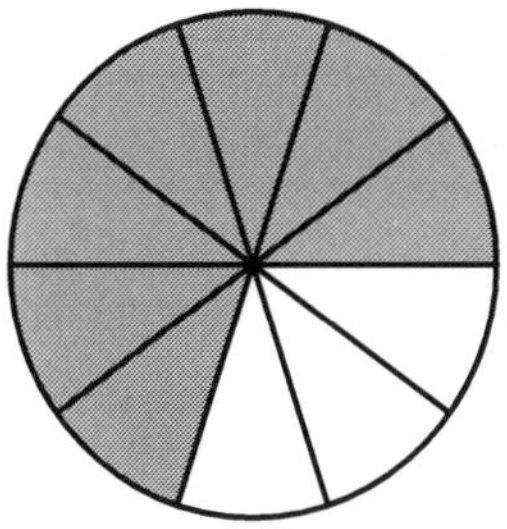

D

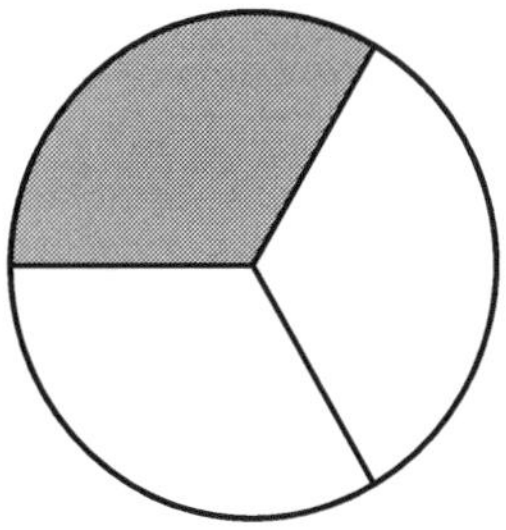

E

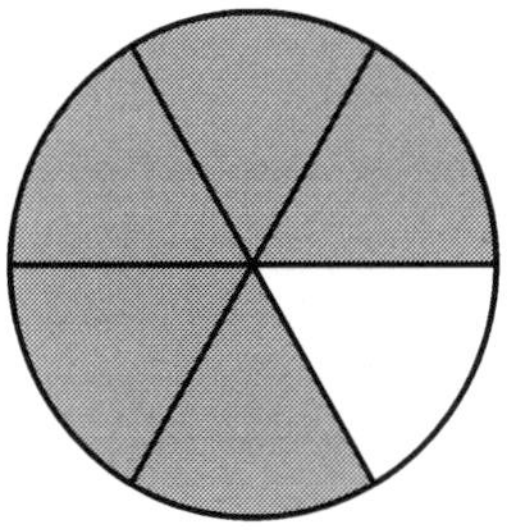

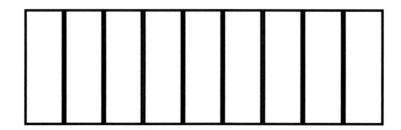

400. How many rectangles should be shaded to fill in one-third of the figure shown above?

    a. 10
    b. 3
    c. 5
    d. 2

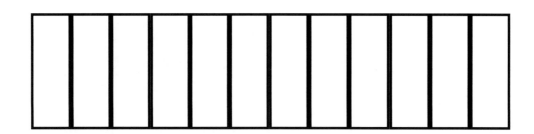

401. How many rectangles should be shaded to fill in one-third of the figure shown above?

    a. 10
    b. 4
    c. 5
    d. 2

402. On the number line shown below, correctly position the following set of fractions above the marks on the number line.

1/10, 5/10, 4/10, 9/10

A

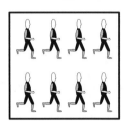

C

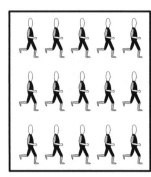

B

D

403. Which is the largest number?

    a. 1/2 of A
    b. 1/2 of B
    c. 1/2 of C
    d. 1/2 of D

404. Which is the smallest number?

    a. 1/4 of A
    b. 1/2 of B
    c. 1/3 of C
    d. 1/4 of D

405. Which is the largest number?

    a. 1/8 of A
    b. 1/3 of B
    c. 1/5 of C
    d. 1/3 of D

A

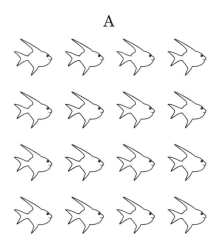

C

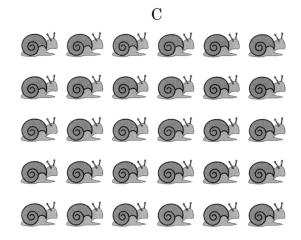

B

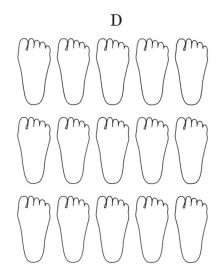

D

406. Which is the largest number?

    a. 1/2 of A
    b. 1/2 of B
    c. 1/2 of C
    d. 1/2 of D

A

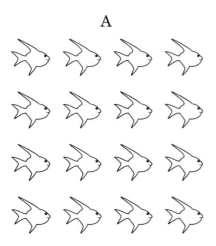

C

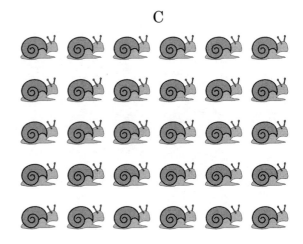

B

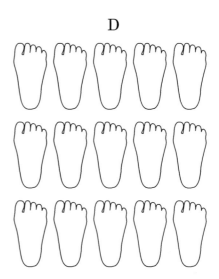

D

407. Which is the largest number?

    a. 1/4 of A
    b. 1/5 of B
    c. 1/6 of C
    d. 1/5 of D

78

A

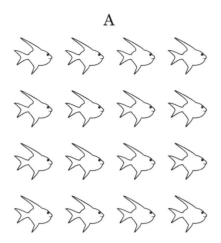

C

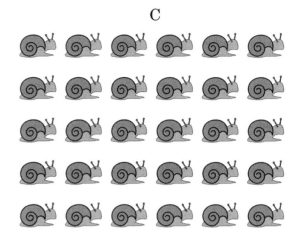

B

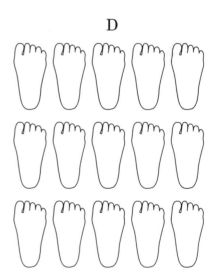

D

408. Which is the smallest number?

    a. 1/4 of A
    b. 1/4 of B
    c. 1/5 of C
    d. 1/5 of D

Arrange the following from SMALLEST to LARGEST.

409. 3/5, 2/5, 4/5, 1/5

    a. 3/5, 2/5, 4/5, 1/5
    b. 1/5, 2/5, 3/5, 4/5
    c. 1/5, 3/5, 2/5, 4/5
    d. 4/5, 2/5, 3/5, 1/5

410. 7/8, 5/8, 3/8, 6/8

    a. 3/8, 5/8, 6/8, 7/8
    b. 3/8, 7/8, 6/8, 5/8
    c. 7/8, 3/8, 5/8, 6/8
    d. 7/8, 6/8, 5/8, 3/8

411. 1/4, 1/2, 1/3, 1/5

    a. 1/4, 1/2, 1/3, 1/5
    b. 1/2, 1/3, 1/4, 1/5
    c. 1/5, 1/3, 1/4, 1/2
    d. 1/5, 1/4, 1/3, 1/2

412. 1/12, 1/20, 1/9, 1/100

    a. 1/12, 1/20, 1/9, 1/100
    b. 1/9, 1/12, 1/100, 1/20
    c. 1/100, 1/20, 1/12, 1/9
    d. 1/20, 1/100, 1/12, 1/9

Complete the following by writing >, <, or = in each of the circles below.

413. $\dfrac{1}{8}$ $\bigcirc$ $\dfrac{1}{4}$

414. $\dfrac{1}{3}$ $\bigcirc$ $\dfrac{1}{2}$

415. $\dfrac{1}{4}$ $\bigcirc$ $\dfrac{1}{5}$

416. $\dfrac{1}{6}$ $\bigcirc$ $\dfrac{1}{9}$

417. Which of the following rules determines how many legs a certain number of dogs would have?

    a. Every four dogs have one leg each.
    b. The number of legs is two times the number of dogs.
    c. The number of legs is four times the number of dogs.
    d. The number of legs is six times the number of dogs.

419. In a book what rule describes the number of the page before the one you are looking at?

    a. The number of the page before is the number of the page that I am looking at minus one.
    b. To find the number of the page before, take the number of the page I am looking at and add one.
    c. The page number is always one more than the page number ahead of it.
    d. The number of the page before minus the page that I am looking at.

418. When Luis was 7, Carlos was 9. Which of the following rules would allow you to figure out Carlos' age if you know Luis'?

    a. Add nine to Luis' age to get Carlos' age.
    b. Carlos' age is Luis' age plus two.
    c. Subtract two from Luis' age to get Carlos' age
    d. Carlos' age is Luis' age plus nine.

420. The rule to determine the number of arms a group of one octopus or more has is

    a. the number of arms is 8 more than the number of octopuses.
    b. the number of octopuses is 8 less than the number of arms.
    c. the number of arms is eight times the number of octopuses.
    d. the number of arms is the number of octopuses divided by eight.

Which operation should be used to solve the problems below?

421. Each bag of apples has 9 apples in it. Kate bought 3 bags. How many bags did Kate buy?

$$3 \_\_\_\_ 9 = 27$$

a. addition (+)
b. subtraction (-)
c. multiplication (x)
d. division (÷)

422. Serena paid $39 for 1 dozen plus 1 ears of corn. How much did she pay for each ear?

$$39 \_\_\_\_ 13 = 3$$

a. addition (+)
b. subtraction (-)
c. multiplication (x)
d. division (÷)

423. Jose collects "How To" books. He has 15 books. He paid $4 for each of the books. How much did he spend all together?

$$\$15 \_\_\_\_ 4 = \$60$$

a. addition (+)
b. subtraction (-)
c. multiplication (x)
d. division (÷)

424. Lee put all his crayons into 3 boxes. He has 72 crayons. How many crayons did he put into each box?

$$72 \_\_\_\_ 3 = 24$$

a. addition (+)
b. subtraction (-)
c. multiplication (x)
d. division (÷)

For the following number sentences choose the question which the number sentence represents.

425. 3 x 4 =

   a. Herman bought 3 cans of tennis balls. Each can had 4 balls in it. How many tennis balls did Herman buy?

   b. Herman spent $3 each for 3 cans of tennis balls with 4 balls in each can. How much did Herman spend?

   c. Herman bought 12 cans of tennis balls. Each can had 3 balls in it. How many tennis balls did Herman buy?

   d. Herman bought 12 tennis balls in 3 cans. How many tennis balls were in each can?

426. $24 ÷ 12 =

   a. Sasha and Niko called each other 12 times yesterday. By the end of the day they had spent $24 in long distance charges. How much did each call cost?

   b. A dictionary costs $12. Ms. Gonzales wanted to buy one for each student in her class. How much would she have to spend altogether?

   c. Sami paid $24 for her bus ride to St. Paul. Sami's son was 9 years old, so she only paid half as much for him. How much did she pay for both of them?

   d. Chicken pieces cost $2 each. How much does one dozen pieces cost?

427. There were 8 students in Mr. Jordan's art class. Each student needed 2 pencils. Which number sentence could be used to find how many pencils the class needed in all?

   a. 8 + 2 =
   b. 8 - 2 =
   c. 8 x 2 =
   d. 8 ÷ 2 =

428. Mr. Fong is making some rings. He will use 3 stones in each ring. He has 21 stones. Which number sentence shows how to find the number of rings Mr. Fong can make?

   a. 21 + 3 =
   b. 21 - 3 =
   c. 21 x 3 =
   d. 21 ÷ 3 =

Solve for s in each of the following problems.

429. $s + s + s = 9$

434. $s \times s = 36$

430. $s \times s = 16$

435. $s + s + s + s = 32$

431. $s + s + s + s = 20$

436. $s + s + s = 21$

432. $s + s = 10$

437. $s \times s = 100$

433. $s + s + s = 18$

438. $s + s + s + s = 28$

In each of the following problems, solve for u.

439. $9 \times u = 99$

440. $u \times 4 = 40$

441. $9 \times u = 81$

442. $u \times 3 = 36$

443. $u \times 2 = 22$

444. $10 \times u = 60$

445. $7 \times u = 84$

446. $12 \times u = 132$

In each of the following problems, solve for n.

447. $n \div 10 = 11$

448. $56 \div n = 7$

449. $n \div 12 = 6$

450. $24 \div n = 2$

451. $80 \div n = 10$

452. $n \div 12 = 5$

453. $32 \div n = 4$

454. $108 \div n = 9$

$$24 \div x = 2$$

455. Which of the following would be the value of x that would make the above equation true?

a. 48
b. 6
c. 12
d. 4

$$s \times 5 \times 2 = 120$$

457. In the above number sentence, $s =$

a. 12.
b. 10.
c. 6
d. 4.

$$4 \times n \times 10 = 80$$

456. In the above number sentence, $n =$

a. 8.
b. 6.
c. 4.
d. 2.

$$3 \times 2 \times u = 42$$

458. In the above number sentence, $u =$

a. 8.
b. 6.
c. 9.
d. 7.

$$4 \times 10 = \boxed{?} \times 5$$

459. Which of the following number should be written in the circle to make the number sentence shown above correct?

    a. 6
    b. 8
    c. 7
    d. 9

$$15 + 45 = \boxed{?} \times 4$$

461. What number should be written in the circle to make the number sentence shown above correct?

$$\blacktriangle + \blacktriangle + \blacktriangle + \blacktriangle = 60$$

460. What number does $\blacktriangle$ stand for in the above number sentence?

    a. 15
    b. 10
    c. 12
    d. 20

462. If $\blacktriangle \times \blacktriangle = \blacklozenge$, then which of the following is TRUE?

    a. $\blacklozenge \times \blacklozenge = \blacktriangle$
    b. $\blacklozenge \times \blacktriangle = \blacktriangle \times \blacktriangle \times \blacktriangle \times \blacktriangle$
    c. $\blacktriangle \times \blacktriangle = \blacklozenge \times \blacktriangle$
    d. $\blacklozenge \times \blacklozenge = \blacktriangle \times \blacktriangle \times \blacktriangle \times \blacktriangle$

GROUP 1: Polygons

GROUP 2: Figures with all sides of equal length

GROUP 3: Figures with two sets of parallel lines

463. Which geometric figure shown below would fit into all three of the above groups?

a.

b.

c.

d.

Think about the three groups of geometric figures described below and then answer the following questions.

> **GROUP 1**: Polygons
>
> **GROUP 2**: Figures with all sides of equal length
>
> **GROUP 3**: Figures with at least one set of parallel lines

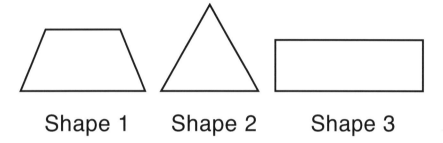

Shape 1   Shape 2   Shape 3

464. Write the numbers of ALL the GROUPS—Group 1, Group 2, or Group 3—in which Shape 1 belongs.

465. Write the numbers of ALL the GROUPS in which Shape 2 belongs.

466. Write the numbers of ALL the GROUPS in which Shape 3 belongs.

467. Name AND draw one figure that does NOT belong in any of the three groups.

468. Name AND draw one figure that belongs in ALL three groups.

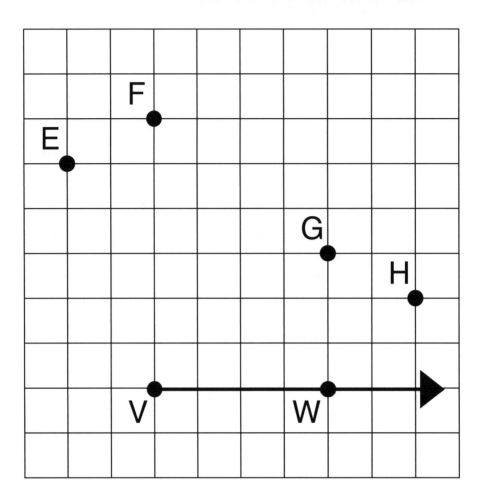

469. Jody connected points V and W to make one side of an angle. Which point should Jody connect to point V in order to make a right angle?

To complete the following problems, you will connect dots on the dot patterns shown below. You will be drawing closed shapes with STRAIGHT SIDES.

470. On the dot pattern labeled Part A, draw a shape that has three angles and three sides.

471. On the dot pattern labeled Part B, draw a shape that has six angles and six sides.

472. On the dot pattern labeled Part C, draw a shape that has four angles and four sides.

473. On the dot pattern labeled Part D, draw a shape that has five angles and five sides.

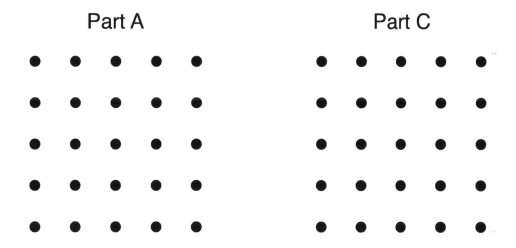

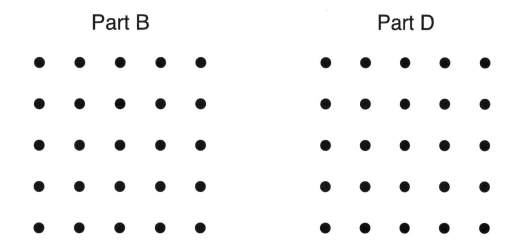

474. Measure the width of the coin to the nearest half inch.

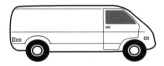

475. Measure the length of the van to the nearest half inch.

476. Measure the height of the cup to the nearest half inch.

a ———————————————

b ————————

c ————————————

d ——————————————————

e —————————

477. Use a ruler to measure line
    d to the nearest half inch.

    line *d* =

480. Use a ruler to measure line
    e to the nearest inch.

    line *e* =

478. Use a ruler to measure line
    b to the nearest inch.

    line *b* =

481. Use a ruler to measure line
    c to the nearest half inch.

    line *c* =

479. Use a ruler to measure line
    a to the nearest half inch.

    line *a* =

482. Use a ruler to measure line
    b to the nearest half inch.

    line *b* =

Each of the figures shown below is a square. The length of one side of each of these figures is given. Find the perimeter of each of these figures.

8 feet

6 feet

3 feet

483.   perimeter =   485.   perimeter =   487.   perimeter =

10 feet

4 feet

2 feet

484.   perimeter =   486.   perimeter =   488.   perimeter =

94

Each of the figures shown below is a rectangle. The length and width of each of these figures is given. Find the perimeter of each of these figures.

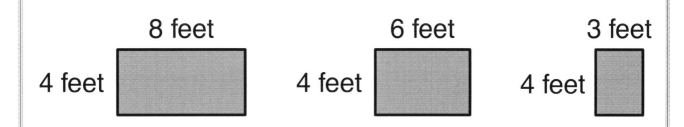

489.   perimeter =   491.   perimeter =   493.   perimeter =

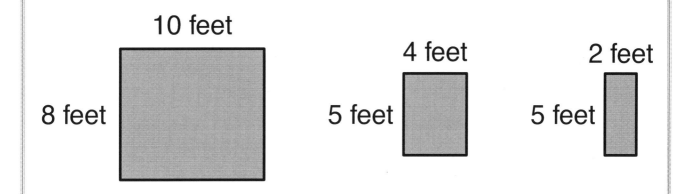

490.   perimeter =   492.   perimeter =   494.   perimeter =

Find the perimeter of each of the triangles shown below.

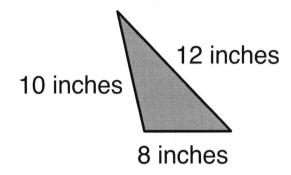

495.   perimeter =

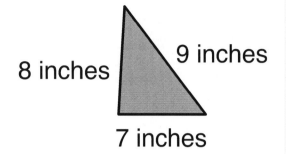

497.   perimeter =

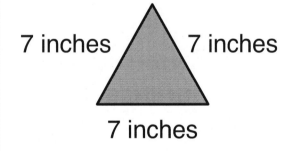

496.   perimeter =

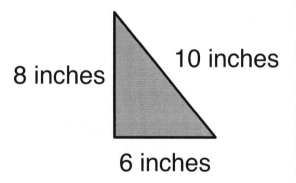

498.   perimeter =

96

50 yards

100 yards

499. A park in the shape of a rectangle is 50 yards wide and 100 yards long. What is the perimeter of the park?

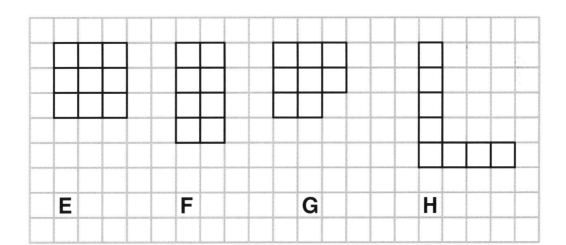

E   F   G   H

500. Which of the figures shown in the above diagram has the LARGEST perimeter?

a. figure E
b. figure F
c. figure G
d. figure H

Indicate the times displayed on the analog clocks shown below.

501. _____

502. _____

503. _____

504. Yesterday morning, Isabel left her house to go to soccer practice at the time shown on the above clock. What time did she leave for practice?

    a. 12:45 a.m.
    b. 11:09 p.m.
    c. 11:40 a.m.
    d. 12:25 p.m.

505. Isabel's practice began at noon. It lasted for 1 1/2 hours. What time was it over?

    a. 12:30 p.m.
    b. 1:15 p.m.
    c. 1:30 p.m.
    d. 1:45 p.m.

Draw in the minute and the hour hands on each of the analog clocks shown below so that they indicate the same time as their corresponding digital clocks.

506.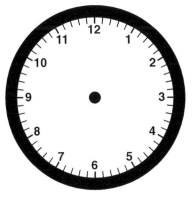

508.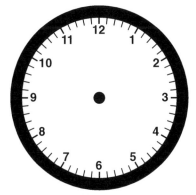

507.

509.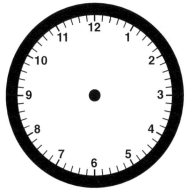

99

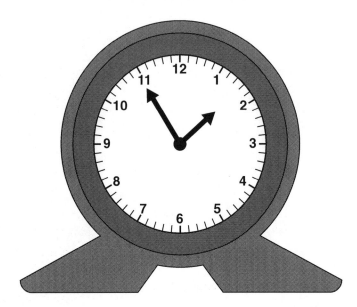

510. Yesterday morning, Nadia left her house to go jogging at the time shown on the above analog clock. She returned home one hour and 45 minutes later. Which of the following digital clocks shows the time that Nadia returned home?

a.

c.

b.

3:35

d.

1:45

100

Use the clock shown below to solve the following problems.

511. What time will it be two hours from the time shown above?

    a. 4:45
    b. 2:45
    c. 3:25
    d. 4:25

512. What time will it be three and one-half hours from the time shown above?

    a. 5:45
    b. 5:25
    c. 5:30
    d. 5:55

513. If the above clock was showing the time in the afternoon, how much time has passed if the time is now 7:00 p.m.?

    a. four hours, thirty-five minutes
    b. three hours
    c. four hours
    d. four hours, forty minutes

514. If the above clock was showing the time in the morning, how much time has passed if the time is now 6:25 a.m.?

    a. three hours
    b. four hours
    c. five hours
    d. six hours

515. Which digital clock shows the same time as the standard clock shown below?

a. **12:15**

c. **1:45**

b. **11:10**

d. **2:20**

516. Camila went to sleep at 10:30 p.m. and woke up the next day at 6:45 a.m. How long did Camila sleep?

  a. three hours, thirty minutes
  b. nine hours, forty-five minutes
  c. eight hours, fifteen minutes
  d. twelve hours

517. Donisha was the leader on his hockey team with 210 penalty minutes. What number best shows the total hours he was penalized?

  a. 2.25
  b. 3.50
  c. 6.00
  d. 3.00

518. Yesterday morning, Sharla left her house to go to soccer practice at the time shown on the above clock. She returned home that afternoon at 3:20 p.m. For how long was Sharla gone?

   a. 3 hours, 20 minutes
   b. 1 hour, 20 minutes
   c. 4 hours
   d. 2 hours, 55 minutes

519. There was a power failure last Thursday at 8:10 a.m. The power wasn't restored until the next day at 9:25 a.m. Which of the following statements BEST describes the period in which there was no power?

   a. The power was out for less than 24 hours.
   b. The power was out for about 12 hours.
   c. The power was out for about 25 hours.
   d. The power was out for more than 48 hours.

Beginning Time   Ending Time

8:10   9:50

520. Victor attends the state university. His Tuesday morning History class begins and ends at the times shown on the above digital clocks. How long is Victor's History class?

   a. 110 minutes
   b. 100 minutes
   c. 90 minutes
   d. 80 minutes

103

521. Juanita started her homework at
7:00 p.m. At 8:15 p.m., she was
50% done. Working at the same
rate, at what time that evening
will Juanita have all of her homework done?

a. 8:30
b. 8:45
c. 9:00
d. 9:30

523. It takes the Cog Railway train
about 1 1/2 hours to travel from
the base station to the top of
Mount Washington. If the train
leaves the base station at
11:00 a.m., about what time
will it reach the top?

a. 11:30 a.m.
b. 12:30 p.m.
c. 1:30 p.m.
d. 2:30 p.m.

522. An airplane left at 3:45 p.m. It
flew for 2 hours and 30 minutes.
What time did the airplane arrive
at its destination?

a. 5:15 p.m.
b. 5:75 p.m.
c. 6:15 p.m.
d. 6:45 p.m.

524. Javier did homework for 1 hour
and 30 minutes. He finished at
8:00 p.m. At what time did he
start his homework?

a. 6:30 p.m.
b. 7:30 p.m.
c. 8:30 p.m.
d. 9:30 p.m.

Convert minutes to hours.

525. 600 minutes =

526. 240 minutes =

527. 480 minutes =

Convert hours to minutes.

531. 6 hours =

532. 9 hours =

533. 3 hours =

Convert minutes to seconds.

528. 5 minutes =

529. 11 minutes =

530. 4 minutes =

Convert seconds to minutes.

534. 120 seconds =

535. 300 seconds =

536. 540 seconds =

How many...

537. minutes are in an hour?

    a. 7
    b. 12
    c. 30
    d. 60

538. hours are in a day?

    a. 24
    b. 12
    c. 30
    d. 60

539. days are in a week?

    a. 7
    b. 12
    c. 30
    d. 60

540. months are in a year?

    a. 7
    b. 12
    c. 30
    d. 60

541. Which is correct?

    a. Every month has 31 days.
    b. Every year has 365 days.
    c. A year is about 52 weeks.
    d. Every minute is 360 seconds.

542. 24 x 7

    a. Seconds in a minute.
    b. Minutes in a day.
    c. Hours in a week.
    d. Hours in a month.

543. Mark found the coins shown above on the floor of his mother's car. Which of the following is the total value of these coins?

    a. 71¢
    b. 91¢
    c. 81¢
    d. 61¢

 −  =

544. Solve the problem shown above.

    a. 15¢
    b. 20¢
    c. 49¢
    d. 24¢

 +   =

545. Solve the problem shown above.

    a. 6¢
    b. 15¢
    c. 35¢
    d. 10¢

546. Dan had 64¢. After he bought a pencil for 29¢, how much money did he have then?

   a. 45¢
   b. 44¢
   c. 35¢
   d. 34¢

547. If a pencil costs 5¢, and you pay for it with a dime, how much change should you receive?

   a. one dime
   b. two pennies
   c. one nickel
   d. one quarter

548. Ted has 3 coins with a total value of 36 cents. What three coins does he have?

   a. three dimes, one penny
   b. one quarter, one nickel, one dime
   c. one quarter, one dime, one penny
   d. one quarter, two pennies

549. Duane had 45¢, then he found 39¢ on the ground. How much money does Duane now have?

550. On Monday Juanita put 30¢ in her bank. The next day she put 41¢ in her bank. How much money did she put in her bank on those two days?

551. When Henry bought a cake, the baker gave him 4 coins in change. If the baker gave Henry 37 cents in change, what were the four coins he received?

   a. one quarter, two nickels, one penny
   b. one quarter, one dime, two pennies
   c. one quarter, two nickels, one dime
   d. one quarter, two pennies, one nickel

552. Steve spent 65 cents ($.65) for a wiffleball and 89 cents ($.89) for a jack set. How much money did he spend in all?

   a. $1.24
   b. $1.54
   c. $1.64
   d. $1.34

553. Jose is buying lunch at school. He wants to buy an ice cream cone for 10 cents ($.10). He has on his tray a carton of milk that costs a nickel and spaghetti that costs 20 cents ($.20). How much will Jose spend for lunch at school if he gets the ice cream cone?

   a. $0.45
   b. $0.30
   c. $0.35
   d. $0.25

554. Shakira bought a pencil for $0.44. She paid for it with $1.00. Which of the following could not be the change that she received?

   a. Two quarters, a nickel, and a penny
   b. Four dimes, three nickels, and a penny
   c. A quarter, a dime, five nickels, and a penny
   d. A quarter, six nickels, and a penny

555. Maria bought a candy bar for $0.62. She paid with a dollar bill. Which would be the fewest coins she could receive for change? Be sure to show all your work.

Stacey needs $3.00 to buy a movie ticket. She checks her "change jar" to see if she has enough money in coins to buy a ticket. Shown below are the coins that Stacey has in her jar.

556. Does Stacey have enough money in coins to buy the movie ticket? Explain your answer.

Remember:

1 penny = $.01

1 nickel = $.05

1 dime = $.10

1 quarter = $.25

110

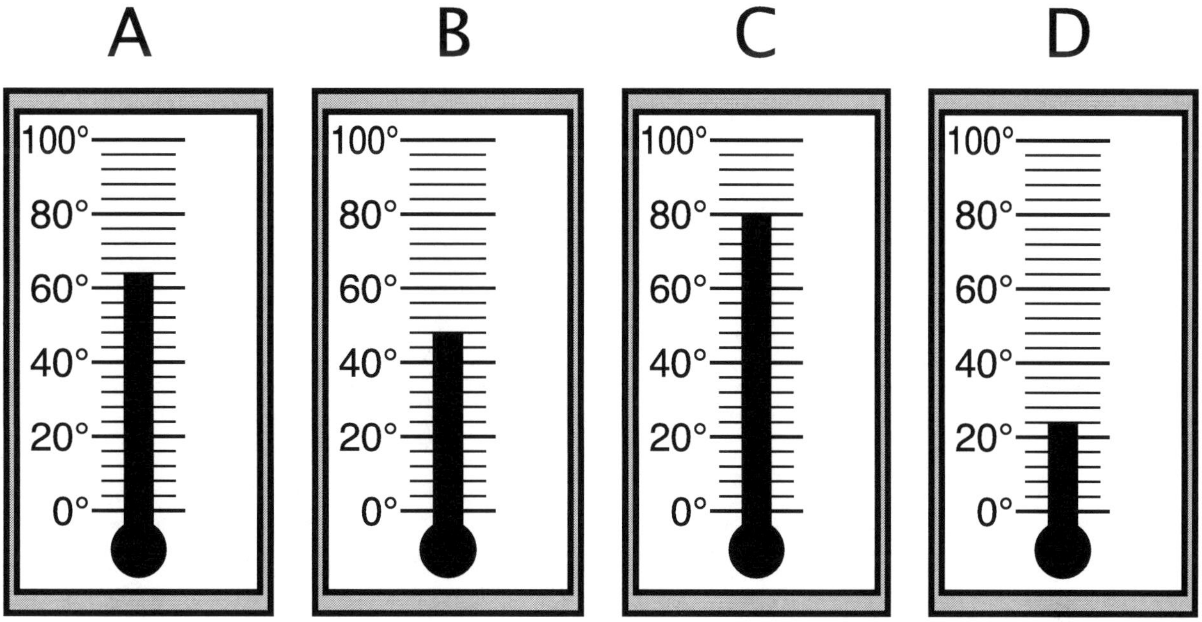

A   B   C   D

Which of the above Celsius thermometers show a temperature of approximately:

557. 62°

    A B C D

558. 23°

    A B C D

559. 81°

    A B C D

560. 50°

    A B C D

111

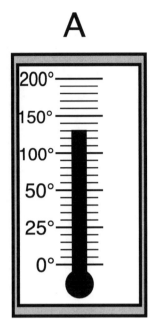
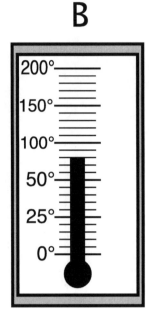
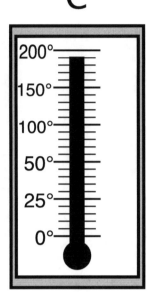
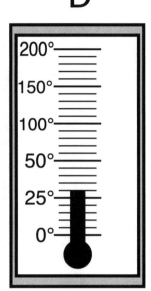

Which of the above Fahrenheit thermometers show a temperature of approximately:

561. 30°

    A B C D

562. 120°

    A B C D

563. 72°

    A B C D

564. 191°

    A B C D

565. Draw a Celsius and a Fahrenheit thermometer. Show each of them at 70°.

The graph below shows how many different kinds of pets were sold at the local pet store this past weekend.

Kind of Pet

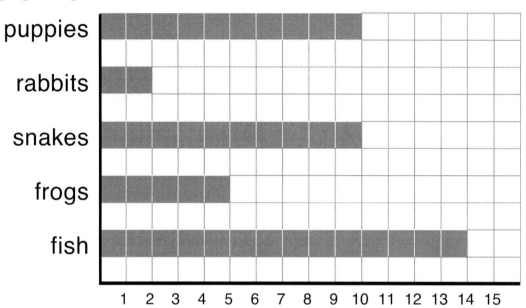

Number Sold

566. According to the graph, how many snakes were sold?

567. According to the graph, how many pets were sold altogether?

114

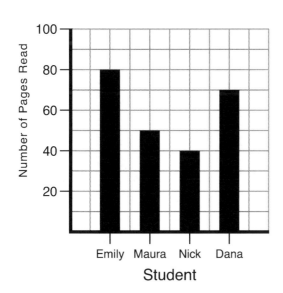

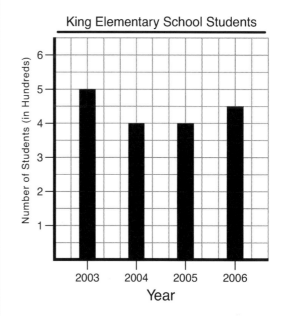

Emily, Maura, Nick, and Dana each have to read the same book for their English class. The above graph shows the number of pages each student has read so far.

568. Which student has read the most number of pages?

569. Which student has read the fewest number of pages?

The above graph shows the number of students that attended King Elementary School each year for the years 2003 through 2006.

570. In which two years was the number of students that attended the school the same?

571. How many students attended the school in 2006?

115

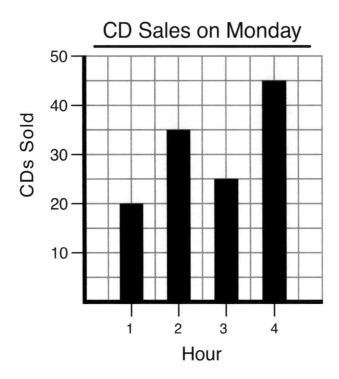

CD Sales on Monday

A store in the mall had a sale on CDs on Monday. The above graph shows the number of CDs sold in the first four hours of the sale.

572.   Altogether, how many CDs were sold in these four hours?

573.   In which hour were the fewest CDs sold?

574.   How many MORE CDs were sold in hour 2 than in hour 3?

    a. 5
    b. 10
    c. 15
    d. 20

For a science project, Candice poured soda into a glass. Once the foam was gone, she counted the bubbles that popped on the top of the soda. She recorded the number of pops each minute for 8 minutes and made the graph below to show the results.

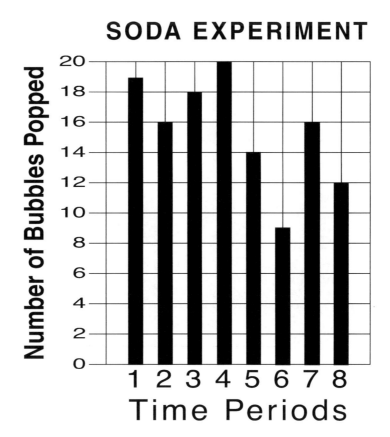

575. Candice's teacher had a question to ask about the results of Candice's project. Which of the following questions would her teacher LEAST LIKELY ask?

    a. Which time period had the most bubbles?
    b. What brand of soda did Candice use?
    c. What was the lowest amount of bubbles for a time period?
    d. How many time periods did she use?

The graph below shows the number of gold medals won by 5 countries in the 1988 Winter Olympics:

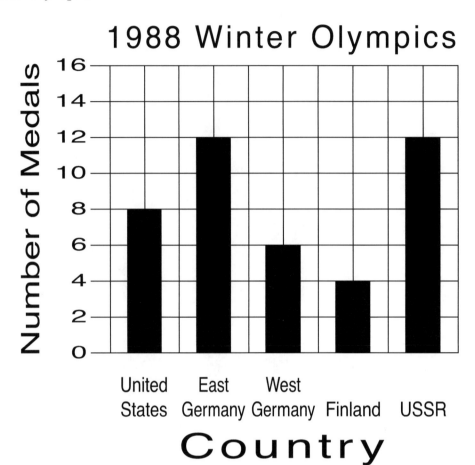

576. Which countries won the same number of gold medals?

    a. United States and West Germany
    b. East Germany and USSR
    c. West Germany and Finland
    d. Finland and USSR

577. Which country won the fewest number of gold medals?

    a. United States
    b. East Germany
    c. West Germany
    d. Finland

118

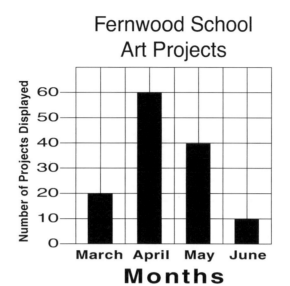

Fernwood School
Art Projects

578. This graph shows the number of art projects from Fernwood School displayed at the local library. According to the graph, how many art projects were displayed altogether?

a. 90
b. 110
c. 130
d. 150

579. In which two months were the greatest number of art projects displayed?

a. March and June
b. April and June
c. April and May
d. March and May

580. In which month were less than 20 art projects displayed?

a. March
b. April
c. May
d. June

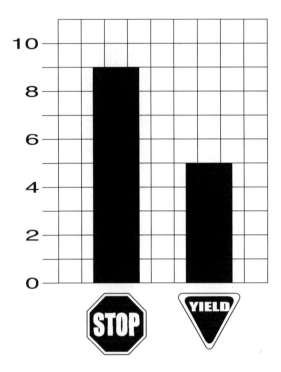

On a field trip, Mr. Chen's students counted the road signs that they saw. When they returned to school, the students made a graph of the number of each kind of sign they saw.

581. How many more stop signs did they count than yield signs?

    a. 3
    b. 4
    c. 5
    d. 6

582. How many road signs did the students count in all?

    a. 28
    b. 24
    c. 14
    d. 10

The third-grade students at Fairway Elementary School voted for their favorite authors. The graph shows the number of students who voted for each author.

583. Which two authors received the most votes?

    a. R.L. Stine and Joanna Cole
    b. Beverly Cleary and Joanna Cole
    c. Roald Dahl and Donald Sobol
    d. Beverly Cleary and Roald Dahl

584. Who received eight or less votes?

    a. R.L. Stine and Joanna Cole
    b. Beverly Cleary and Joanna Cole
    c. Roald Dahl and Donald Sobol
    d. Beverly Cleary and Roald Dahl

Tabitha counted the number of houses on each street in her neighborhood. She displayed her totals in the table shown below.

Street Name	No. of Houses
Hill Street	18
Elm Street	20
Pleasant Avenue	15
Roberts Road	10
Forest Road	4

585. Which of the following graphs correctly shows Tabitha's table?

a.
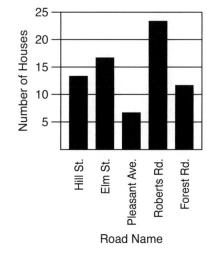

c.
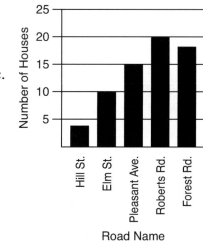

b.
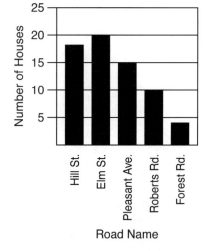

d.
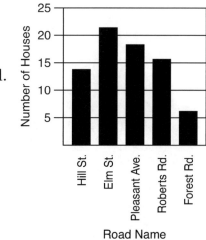

122

A few students at Lockwood Grammar School kept track of the number of days they were absent from school. Their results are in the tally chart shown below.

Days Absent from School	
Wanda	IIII
Steve	HHL II
Eric	HHL
Jean	III
Stella	II

586. Create a bar graph that shows the same data as in the tally chart. Be sure to label your graph.

Yogurt Sales

Day of the Week

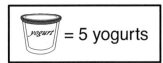 = 5 yogurts

587. Last week, the Carter Elementary School cafeteria kept track of their yogurt sales. This data is shown in the above pictograph. Create a bar graph that would show this data.

124

588. Brixton Elementary School held a fundraiser. The first grade raised a total of $350.00. The second grade raised seventy dollars less than the first grade. The third grade raised a total of $315.00. The fourth grade raised forty-five dollars more than the third grade. Which of the following tables correctly shows the amount of money each grade raised?

a.

Grade	Money Raised
1	$350.00
2	$420.00
3	$360.00
4	$315.00

c.

Grade	Money Raised
1	$280.00
2	$350.00
3	$315.00
4	$360.00

b.

Grade	Money Raised
1	$350.00
2	$280.00
3	$315.00
4	$270.00

d.

Grade	Money Raised
1	$350.00
2	$280.00
3	$315.00
4	$360.00

125

How Students Get to School	
Ride a Bicycle	5
Take the Bus	12
Go by Car	6
Walk	2

589. Janet took a survey of her class. She asked each student how he or she gets to school. Her results are shown in the above table. According to her results, which statement below is NOT true?

a. More students go by car than take the bus.
b. More students ride a bike and walk than go by car.
c. More students take the bus than either walk or go by car.
d. More students ride a bike to school than walk.

The table below shows the number of students in after-school programs at Vargas Elementary School.

After-School Program	Grade					
	K	1	2	3	4	5
Art	32	26	25	29	40	27
Sports	24	20	38	31	23	29

590. How many more students in all are in the art program than in the sports program?

a. 8 students
b. 11 students
c. 14 students
d. 17 students

The chart below lists the possible ways of scoring points in a high school football game and the point values for each way of scoring.

Method of Scoring	Point Value
Touchdown	6 points
Field Goal	3 points
Safety	2 points
Two-Point Conversion	2 points
Extra Point	1 point

Jeff and Tim play high school football. The table below shows how each of the boys scored points during this past football season.

	Jeff	Tim
Number of Touchdowns	8	1
Number of Field Goals	0	9
Number of Safeties	1	0
No. of 2-Point Conversions	1	0
Number of Extra Points	0	17

591. Determine the total number of points that each boy scored.

Jeff's points: _____

Tim's points: _____

Sandy is the assistant manager at a small video store. She kept track of the number of movies that were rented over the last four weeks by movie type. Her results are shown in the table below.

Type of Movie	Number Rented			
	Week 1	Week 2	Week 3	Week 4
Action	1	2	0	1
Comedy	5	4	7	6
Drama	4	2	2	0
Science Fiction	0	1	0	0

592. In which week were the FEWEST movies rented?

    a. week 1
    b. week 2
    c. week 3
    d. week 4

593. What type of movie was rented the MOST OFTEN over this four-week period?

    a. action movies
    b. comedies
    c. dramas
    d. science fiction movies

A survey was done to determine the number of students in after-school programs at Newton Elementary School. Each grade has 20 students, and the after school programs they are in are shown below.

Grade 1

art	sports
art	art
sports	sports
sports	art
art	sports
sports	art
sports	sports
art	art
sports	sports
art	art

Grade 2

sports	art
sports	art
sports	sports
art	art
sports	sports
art	sports
sports	sports
art	sports
sports	art
sports	art

Grade 3

art	art
sports	art
art	art
art	sports
art	art
sports	sports
art	sports
sports	art
art	art
art	sports

594. Create a frequency table to display the information shown above.

The pictograph below shows the number of books in Mrs. Morgan's classroom.

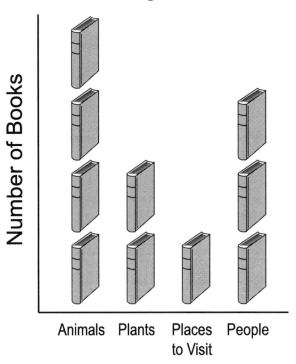

Mrs. Morgan's Books

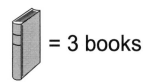 = 3 books

595. Which of the following questions can be answered using the information shown in the above pictograph?

    a. What grade does Mrs. Morgan teach?
    b. How many books about sports are in Mrs. Morgan's classroom?
    c. How many books about people are in Mrs. Morgan's classroom?
    d. How many pages are in Mrs. Morgan's books?

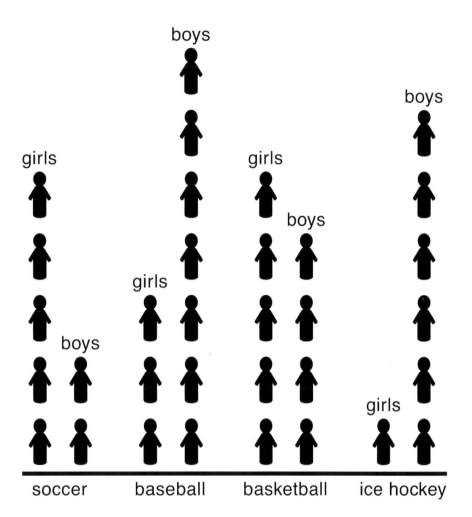

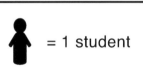 = 1 student

Each boy and girl in Ms. Weston's third-grade class voted for his or her favorite sport. The results are shown the above pictograph.

596. Which sport received the MOST votes?

    a. soccer
    b. baseball
    c. basketball
    d. ice hockey

Use the pictograph shown below to solve the following problems.

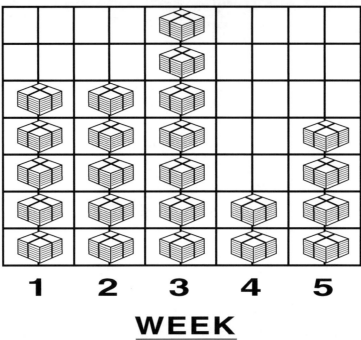

Newspaper Recycled in Mr. Monroe's Class

1   2   3   4   5

WEEK

Each [image] equals 25 pounds of newspaper.

597. How many pounds of newspaper were recycled in week 4?

598. In which two weeks were the SAME amounts of newspaper recycled?

Gina's parents bought her a new bicycle for her birthday. The pictograph below shows how many miles Gina rode her new bicycle in the first three weeks she had it.

Gina's Bicycle Riding

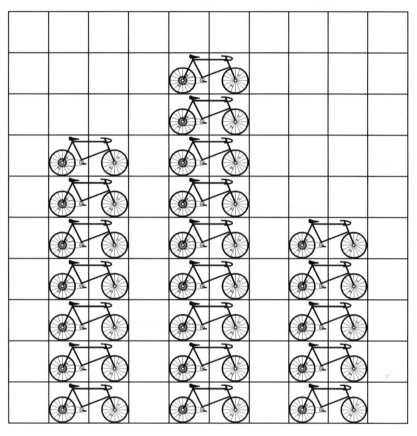

Week 1   Week 2   Week 3

1 🚲 = 5 miles

599. How many miles did Gina ride her bicycle in the third week?

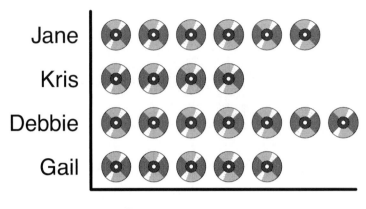

1 ⊙ = 5 CDs

The above pictograph shows the number of CDs owned by Jane, Kris, Debbie, and Gail.

600.   Who owns the most CDs?

601.   How many CDs does Jane own?

602.   How many MORE CDs than Kris does Gail own?

        a. 20
        b. 15
        c. 15
        d. 5

603.   How many CDs do Jane and Kris own combined?

        a. 40
        b. 50
        c. 55
        d. 60

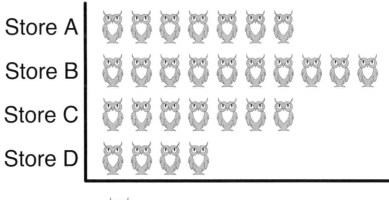

Store A

Store B

Store C

Store D

1 🦉 = 8 owls

Gordon the Owl is one of the more popular items sold at four different toy stores. The above pictograph shows the number of Gordon the Owl sales last month.

604.   Which two stores sold the SAME number of owls?

605.   How many owls did Store B sell?

606.   How many MORE owls did Store A sell than Store D?

   a. 32
   b. 24
   c. 16
   d. 8

607.   How many owls did Store C and Store D sell combined?

   a. 88
   b. 96
   c. 104
   d. 112

135

The graph below shows how many cars were washed each hour by the soccer team.

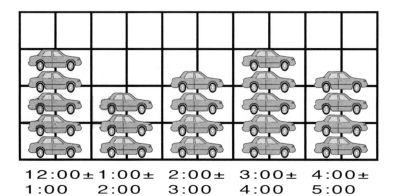

Car Wash Times

Each Represents 5 Cars

608. How many cars did the team wash from 1:00 to 3:00?

   a. 3
   b. 7
   c. 15
   d. 35

609. How many cars did the team wash from 3:00 to 5:00?

   a. 9
   b. 25
   c. 35
   d. 45

610. If the team charged $3.00 to wash each car, how much did they earn from 4:00 to 5:00?

   a. $12.00
   b. $15.00
   c. $20.00
   d. $60.00

136

Mrs. Miller's class received letters from people in a nursing home. The class made a graph of the number of letters they received each week.

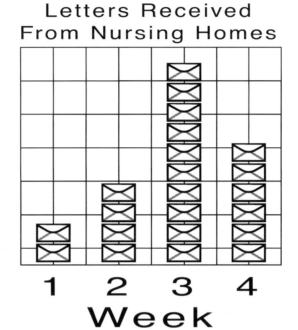

Letters Received From Nursing Homes

Week

Each ✉ Represents 3 Letters

611. How many letters did they receive during Week 2?

    a. 12
    b. 7
    c. 6
    d. 4

612. According to the graph, how many letters did they receive altogether?

    a. 72
    b. 66
    c. 60
    d. 57

Christy is the coach of the soccer team at King Elementary School. She drives the team to and from games in the school van. The pictograph below shows the number of miles Christy drove the soccer team in September, October, and November of last year.

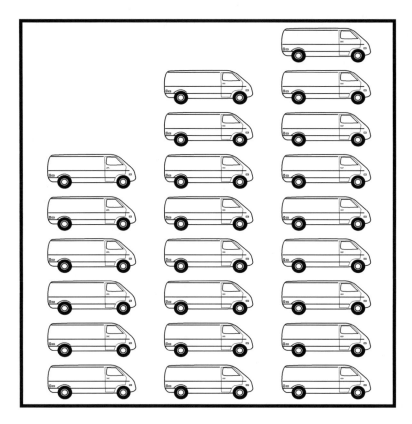

September   October   November
Months

One  = 10 miles.

613. What is the total number of miles that Christy drove the soccer team in these three months?

    a. 300 miles
    b. 250 miles
    c. 230 miles
    d. 270 miles

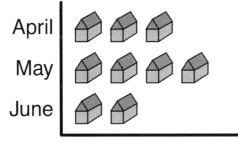

April
May
June
1 = ? houses

614. In the months of April, May, and June, Bruce painted 90 houses. What would one have to equal in the above pictograph for the total number of houses that Bruce painted to be 90?

a. 9 houses
b. 10 houses
c. 11 houses
d. 12 houses

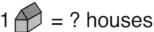

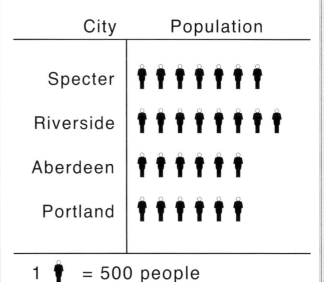

City
Population
Specter
Riverside
Aberdeen
Portland
1 = 500 people

615. The above pictograph shows the population of five towns. According to the pictograph, how many people live in the MOST POPULATED town?

a. 3,000
b. 4,000
c. 2,000
d. 3.500

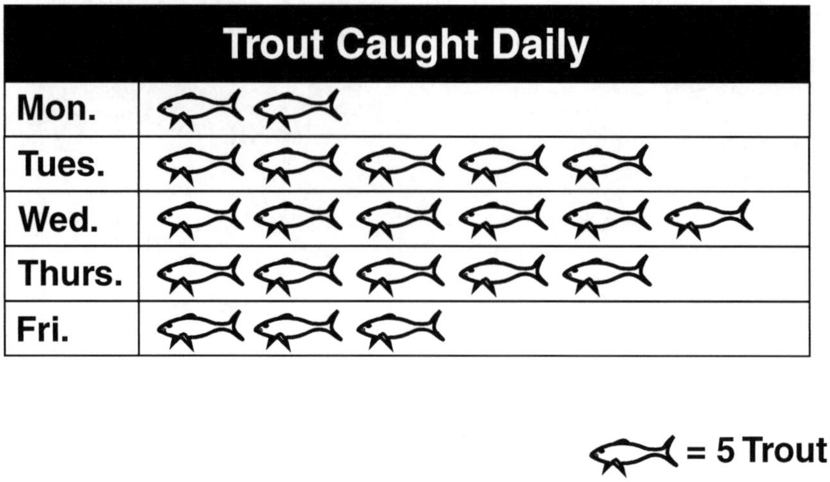

Trout Caught Daily	
Mon.	🐟 🐟
Tues.	🐟 🐟 🐟 🐟 🐟
Wed.	🐟 🐟 🐟 🐟 🐟 🐟
Thurs.	🐟 🐟 🐟 🐟 🐟
Fri.	🐟 🐟 🐟

🐟 = 5 Trout

616. Based on the information in the pictograph shown above, on which days were the SAME amount of fish caught?

617. How many trout were caught on Wednesday?

    a. 5
    b. 6
    c. 25
    d. 30

618. How many more trout were caught on Thursday than on Monday?

    a. 3
    b. 15
    c. 25
    d. 40

Vashti's third-grade class held a muffin sale. The class sold 30 muffins on Wednesday, 20 muffins on Thursday, and 35 muffins on Friday.

619. Given the above information, make a pictograph. Be sure to label your pictograph.

Number of Fish in Fish Tank

Rachel ⌒⌒⌒ ⌒⌒⌒ ⌒⌒⌒

Grace ⌒⌒⌒ ⌒⌒⌒

Laura ⌒⌒⌒ ⌒⌒⌒ ⌒⌒⌒ ⌒⌒⌒

⌒⌒⌒ = 4 fish

620. Which of the following bar graphs BEST represents the information shown in the above pictograph?

a.

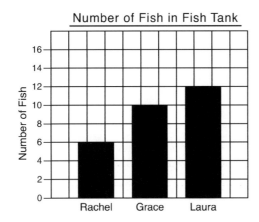

c.

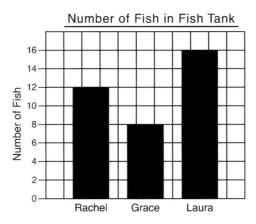

b.

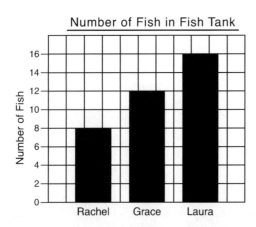

d.

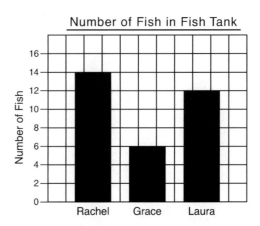

142

Five people collect toy cars as shown in the table below.

Name	Number of Toy Cars
Annette	51
Hector	55
Hannah	30
Craig	25
Katie	73

621. Which of the following graphs BEST displays the information in the table?

a.
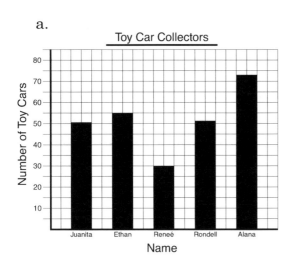

c.
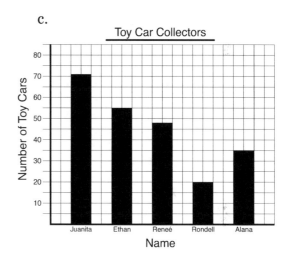

b.
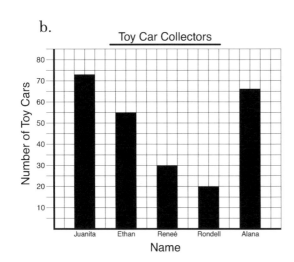

d.
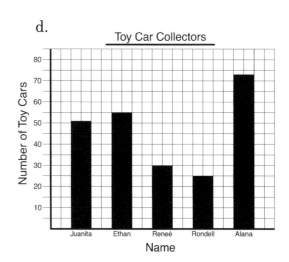

143

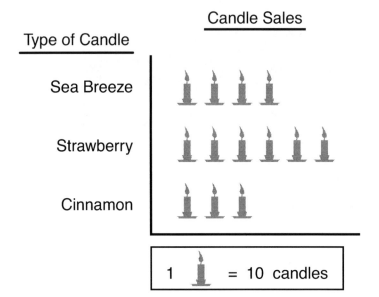

622. The above pictograph shows the number of three types of candles sold by a candle shop in the mall this past weekend. Create a bar graph that would accurately display this information. Be sure to label your graph and to use a correct scale.

Seth and Ian played 25 games of checkers. Seth won the first 4 games. Then Ian won 2 games. Then Seth won 4 games, and Ian won 3 games. Then Seth won 2 games, and Ian won 6 games. The next 2 games were tied. Then each boy won one more game. How many games did each boy win?

623. Which of the following pictographs best shows the solution to the above problem?

a.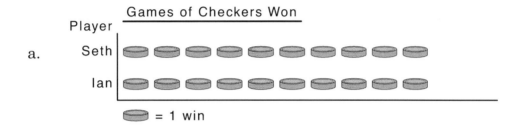

b.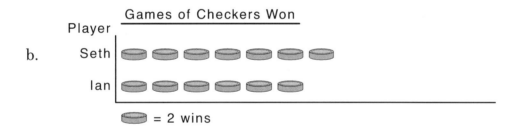

c.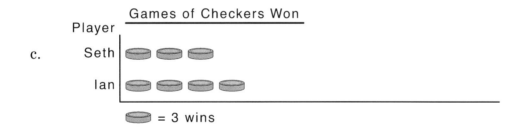

d.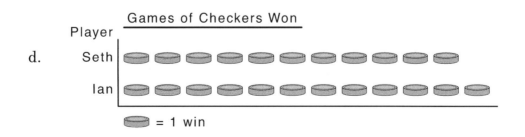

145

The graph below shows the number of quarters in Misha's piggy bank at the end of each week.

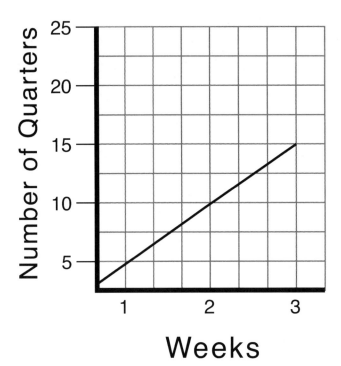

624. What is the VALUE of Misha's quarters at the end of Week 3?

    a. $15.00
    b. $3.75
    c. $3.00
    d. $2.25

625. If Misha continues to save at the same rate, HOW MANY quarters will be in her bank at the end of the fifth week?

    a. 9
    b. 35
    c. 25
    d. 14

The graph shows the height of a brother and sister from January 1, 2000, to January 1, 2001.

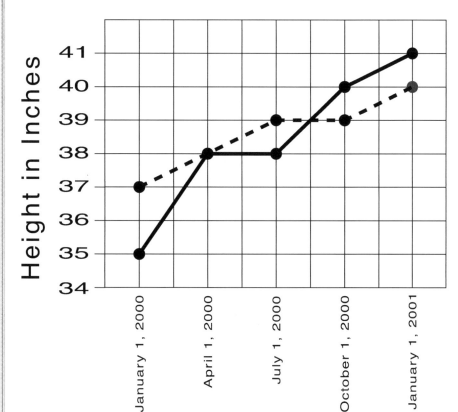

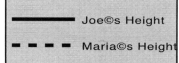

626. On which date were Joe and his sister the SAME height?

    a. January 1, 2000
    b. April 1, 2000
    c. July 1, 2000
    d. October 1, 2000

627. How tall was Joe on October 1, 2000?

    a. 38 inches
    b. 40 inches
    c. 39 inches
    d. 34 inches

628. Each graph below shows the growth of a different plant. Which graph represents the plant that grew the FASTEST?

a.

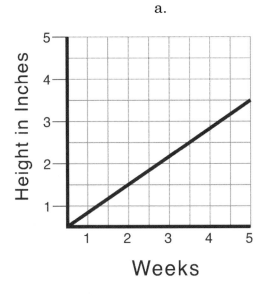

c.

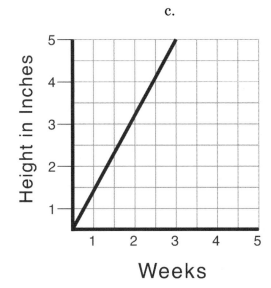

b.

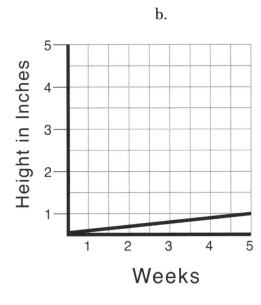

d.

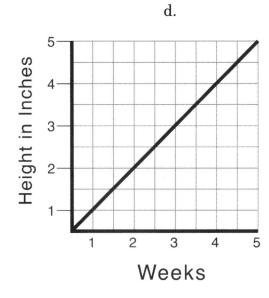

The graph below shows the number of quarters in Wendy's "quarters jar" at the end of each week.

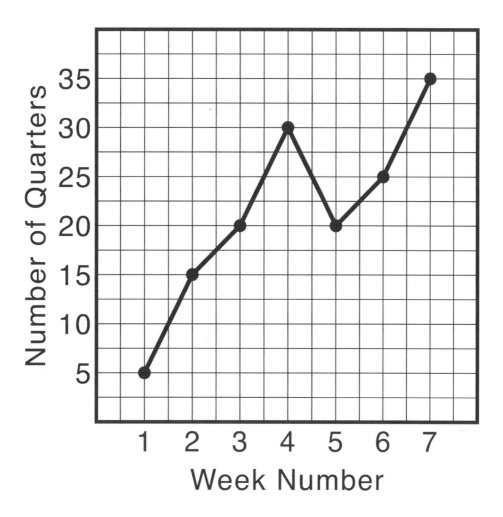

629. In which two weeks did Wendy's jar contain the SAME amount of quarters?

    a. week 1 and week 7
    b. week 3 and week 5
    c. week 4 and week 6
    d. week 2 and week 4

149

About The Practice Tests

These practice tests are designed to prepare students for the Grade 3 Minnesota Comprehensive Assessment II (MCA-III) mathematics test. They contain problems dealing with number sense; patterns, functions, and algebra; data analysis, statistics, and probability; and spatial sense, geometry, and measurement. The problems included in the practice tests are chosen to best represent those that will appear on the Grade 3 MCA-III mathematics test.

To simulate the actual test-taking experience, each part of the practice tests will be timed. Answers to multiple-choice problems will be filled in by the students on the answer grid located on page T29 for the Pretest and on page T59 for the Posttest.

151 PLEASE GO ON TO THE NEXT PAGE.

This part of the test contains twenty-one multiple-choice problems and one constructed-response problem. Be sure to show all your work when solving the constructed-response problem. Any calculations may be written directly on the pages in this section or in the additional work space on pages T25 through T28. You may also use this additional work space if you need more room to write your answer to the constructed-response problem. Your answer to this problem must be clearly labeled regardless of where it appears in the practice test.

If you cannot solve a problem, go on to the next one. If you have time, you may go back and try to solve any problems that you skipped *in this section only*.

You have **seventy-five minutes** to complete this part of the test.

Calculators ARE NOT allowed for this part of the test!

9,000 + 200 + 80 + 6

1. How would the above number be written in standard form?

   a. 9,826
   b. 9,628
   c. 9,286
   d. 9,862

3. If 6 x 9 x 15 = 810, then 15 x 9 x 6 =

   a. 540.
   b. 605.
   c. 980.
   d. 810.

2. Maggie found the total number of stars shown in the above diagram by saying, "7 + 7 + 7 + 7 + 7 = 35." Which of the following expressions can also be used to find the number of stars in the diagram?

   a. 7 + 5
   b. 5 x 7
   c. (7 - 5) x 5
   d. 30 x 5

T2 **PLEASE GO ON TO THE NEXT PAGE.**

4. Clea was born in 1980. When she was twenty-two years old, she graduated college. Nine years later, she opened her own medical practice. Which of the following number sentences could be used to determine the year Clea started her own practice?

a. 1980 - 22 + 9
b. 1980 + 22 - 9
c. 1980 - 22 - 9
d. 1980 + 22 + 9

9 + 6 + 4 + 10 + 2 = 31

5. Ed wants to find another way to write the number sentence shown above. Which of the following is another correct way to write this number sentence?

a. 6 - 4 - 10 - 2 - 9 = 31
b. 6 - 4 + 10 - 2 + 9 = 31
c. 9 + 2 - 6 - 4 + 10 = 31
d. 6 + 4 + 10 + 2 + 9 = 31

6. Paula bought a pair of jeans for $26.00 and a sweater for $53.00. ABOUT how much did she spend on the two items altogether?

a. a little less than $70.00
b. a little more than $80.00
c. a little less than $80.00
d. a little more than $70.00

7. The Northeast Basketball League has twelve teams. Each team has ten players. Which of the following could be used to find the total number of players in this league?

a. 12 x 12
b. 12 x 10
c. 10 x 10
d. 12 + 10

PLEASE GO ON TO THE NEXT PAGE.

8.   Which of the following diagrams does NOT show a rotation?

        a.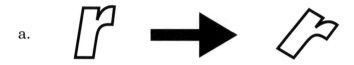

        b.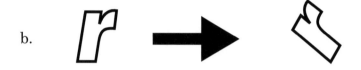

        c.

        d.

T4   **PLEASE GO ON TO THE NEXT PAGE.**

Each number in Set W is paired with a number in Set X. The relationship for each pair of numbers is the same.

Set W	Set X
2	9
6	13
10	17
14	?

9.   If the number in Set W is 14, how will you find its paired number in Set X?

   a. Add 7 to 17.
   b. Add 7 to 14.
   c. Multiply 10 by 7.
   d. Multiply 14 by 7.

10.   Kendra uses one yard of ribbon to make six bows. How much ribbon is used for each bow?

   a. one foot
   b. six inches
   c. ten inches
   d. four inches

11.   Which of the following shows the number 497 in expanded notation?

   a. 4 x 100 +
      9 x 1 +
      7 x 10

   b. 4 x 100 +
      9 x 100 +
      7 x 100

   c. 4 x 100 +
      9 x 10 +
      7 x 1

   d. 4 x 1 +
      9 x 10 +
      7 x 100

12.   Which of the following is TRUE about the whole number 687?

   a. It is greater than five hundred.
   b. It is less than eight hundred.
   c. It is between six hundred and seven hundred.
   d. all of the above

T5   **PLEASE GO ON TO THE NEXT PAGE.**

13. If the stack of books shown above is four feet high, then ABOUT how tall is the camel?

a. 3 feet
b. 5 feet
c. 8 feet
d. 12 feet

14. In which of the following pairs of numbers is the first number 100 less than the second number?

a. 579 and 879
b. 279 and 1,279
c. 979 and 1,079
d. 279 and 179

15. Which of the following numbers means the same as 8,000 + 700 + 90 + 3?

a. 8,973
b. 8,793
c. 8,739
b. 8,937

T6   PLEASE GO ON TO THE NEXT PAGE.

Alice is learning about the planets in her science class. So far, she has learned about five of the nine planets.

Planets in Our Solar System

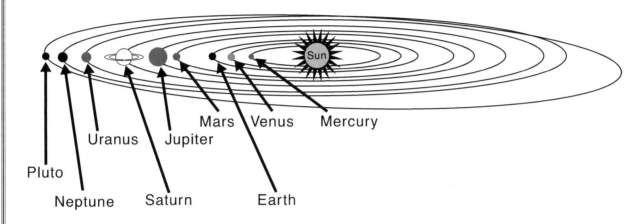

16. Which of the following could be used to find the number of planets that Alice has NOT yet studied?

    a. $9 \div \square = 5$
    b. $9 - 5 = \square$
    c. $5 \times \square = 9$
    d. $\square - 5 = 9$

T7   **PLEASE GO ON TO THE NEXT PAGE.**

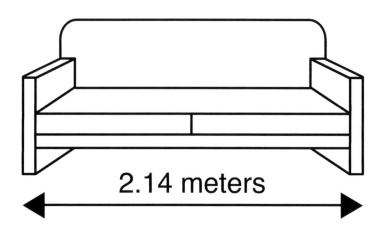

2.14 meters

17. The couch shown in the above diagram is 2.14 meters long. How many centimeters long is this couch?

    a. 21.4 centimeters
    b. 214 centimeters
    c. 2,140 centimeters
    d. 21,400 centimeters

18. Which of the following fish would MOST LIKELY be next in the pattern shown above?

    a.   b.   c.   d.

 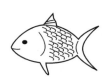 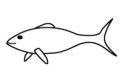 

| 1 | 2 | 3 | 4 | 5 | 6 | 7 | 8 | 9 | 10 | 11 | 12 | 13 | 14 | 15 | 16 |

centimeters

19. Maggie's kitchen floor is made using square tiles. The above diagram shows the size of one of these tiles. How long is one side of one of these tiles?

   a. 16 centimeters
   b. 14 centimeters
   c. 12 centimeters
   d. 10 centimeters

T9 PLEASE GO ON TO THE NEXT PAGE.

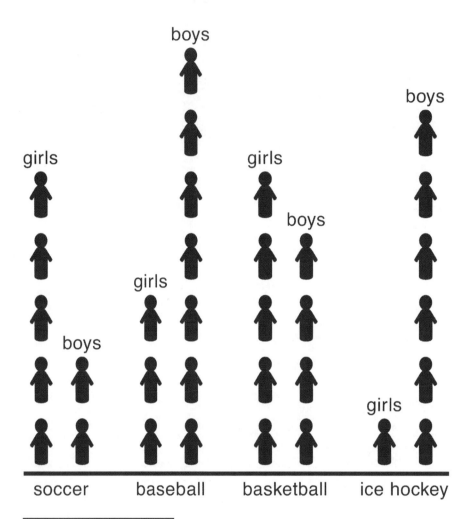

= 1 student

Each boy and girl in Ms. Weston's third-grade class voted for his or her favorite sport. The results are shown the above pictograph.

20.   Which sports did the girls like best?

a. soccer and baseball
b. baseball and hockey
c. soccer and basketball
d. baseball and ice hockey

T10   **PLEASE GO ON TO THE NEXT PAGE.**

21. Which of the following diagrams shows the multiplication fact **5 x 4**?

a.

c.

b.

d.

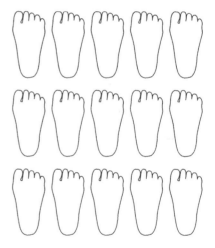

T11 **PLEASE GO ON TO THE NEXT PAGE.** ⬤➡

22.

If 1  = equals one, solve

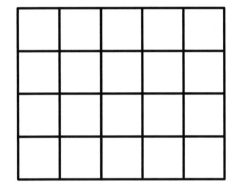 X 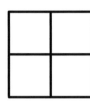 =

T12 **PLEASE STOP! YOU HAVE REACHED THE END OF PART ONE.** STOP!

This part of the test contains twenty-one multiple-choice problems and one constructed-response problem. Be sure to show all your work when solving the constructed-response problem. Any calculations may be written directly on the pages in this section or in the additional work space on pages T25 through T28. You may also use this additional work space if you need more room to write your answer to the constructed-response problem. Your answer to this problem must be clearly labeled regardless of where it appears in the practice test.

If you cannot solve a problem, go on to the next one. If you have time, you may go back and try to solve any problems that you skipped *in this section only*.

If you complete Part Two of the test, you CANNOT return to any previous parts to work on problems you have either skipped over or failed to complete.

You have **seventy-five minutes** to complete this part of the test.

Calculators ARE NOT allowed for this part of the test!

23. Which set of objects below shows the same pattern as AABAABAAB?

a.

b.

c.

d.

22, 21, 19, 16, 12, ___

24. What number would come next in the pattern shown above?

    a. 10
    b. 8
    c. 7
    d. 5

25. One day, a bookstore got 279 copies of a new book. They sold 186 copies during the first week. Which of the following could be used to determine the number of books that they have left?

    a. 279 x 186
    b. 279 + 186
    c. 279 - 186
    d. 279 ÷ 186

T14 PLEASE GO ON TO THE NEXT PAGE.

26. Each graph below shows the growth of a different plant. Which graph represents the plant that grew one inch per week?

a.

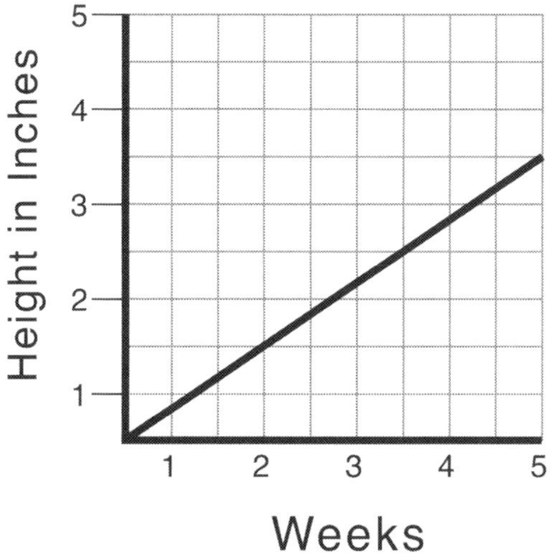

c.

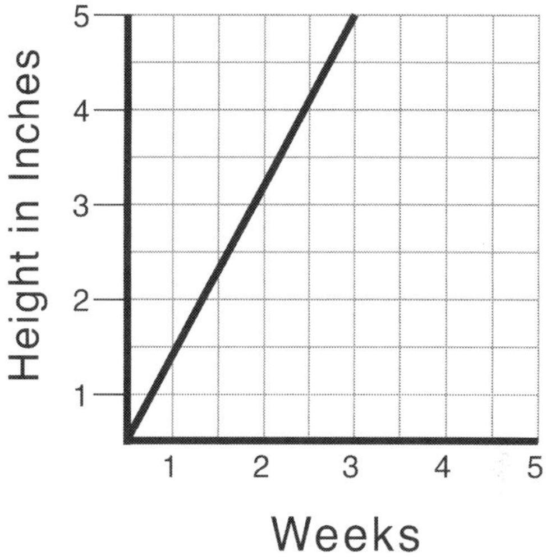

b.

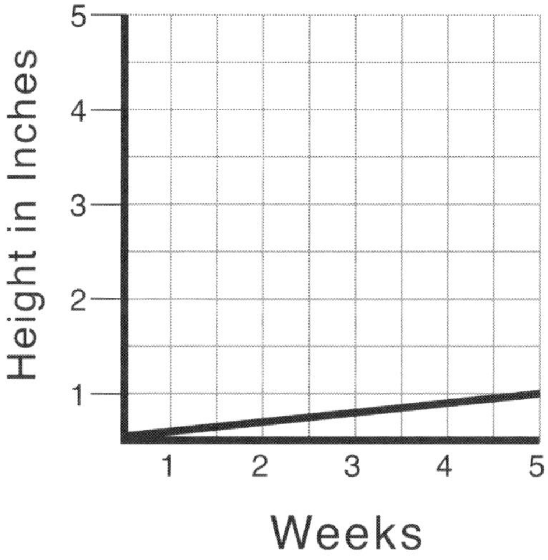

d.

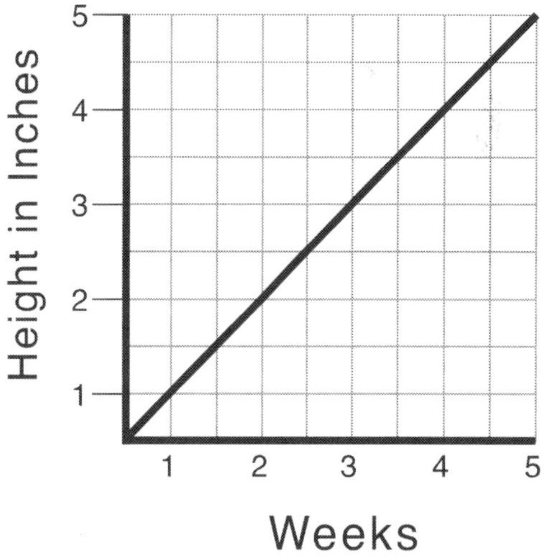

T15   PLEASE GO ON TO THE NEXT PAGE.

The graph below shows the number of quarters in Wendy's "quarters jar" at the end of each week.

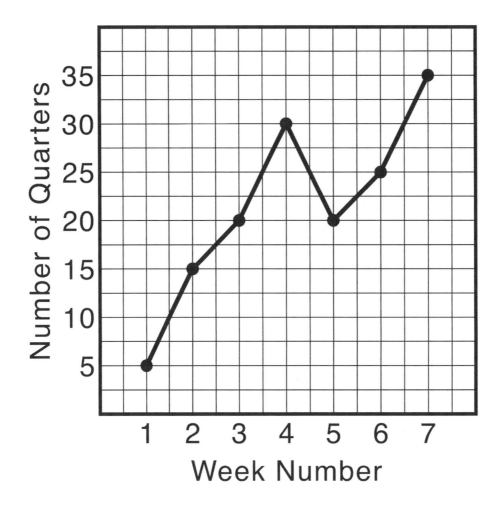

27. In which week did Wendy's jar contain less quarters than the week before?

    a. week 7
    b. week 5
    c. week 6
    d. week 3

T16   **PLEASE GO ON TO THE NEXT PAGE.**

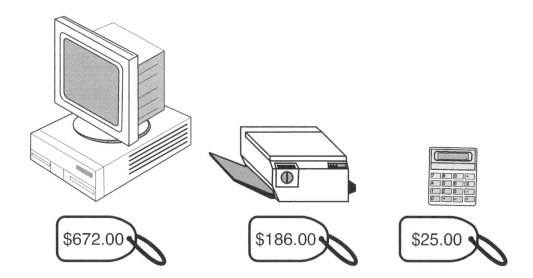

$672.00 $186.00 $25.00

28. Leon bought the above items for his home office at the prices shown. Altogether, how much money did Leon spend on these three items?

a. $883.00
b. $946.00
c. $973.00
d. $865.00

10, 8, 11, 9, 12, 10, 13, 11, ?

29. Which of the following would be the next number in the above pattern?

a. 9
b. 12
c. 14
d. 15

30. Which of the following means the same as 452?

a. 40 + 5 + 2
b. 500 + 40 + 2
c. 400 + 20 + 5
d. 400 + 50 + 2

T17

H. •   •J

•
I

31. Which of the following shapes would be made if the points shown in the above diagram were connected by line segments?

    a. a square
    b. a triangle
    c. a pentagon
    d. a rectangle

32. What time is shown on the above clock?

    a. 2:30
    b. 2:00
    c. 6:30
    d. 4:15

33. Wilson Elementary school had a party. Each student in the third grade brought in two dozen cookies. If there were 49 students in the third grade, then how many dozen cookies were brought in by the third grade students?

    a. 98
    b. 588
    c. 28
    d. 168

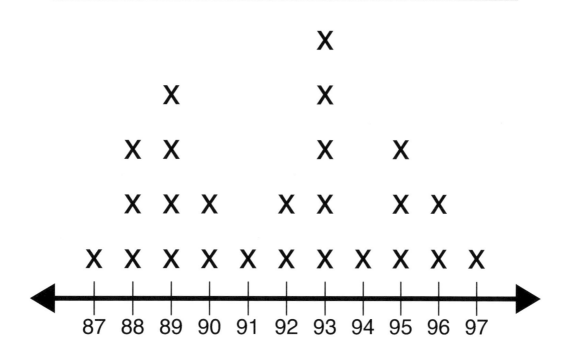

34. The above line plot shows twenty-five third-grade students' scores on their most recent math test. Each **X** represents one student. According to the line plot, how many students scored 93 or higher on this test?

a. 17
b. 10
c. 15
d. 12

T19 PLEASE GO ON TO THE NEXT PAGE.

Test Scores Tally Chart	
100-90	IIII
89-80	IIII IIII II
79-70	IIII
69-60	IIII
59-50	II

35. Which figure below has the SAME number of sides as the figure shown above?

a.

b.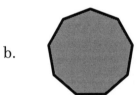

c.

d.

36. The students in Mrs. Fleming's third-grade class took a math test. The test scores are shown in the above tally chart. If the score needed to pass this test is 70 or higher, how many students passed this test?

a. 10
b. 21
c. 6
d. 12

37. There are 177 papers to fold. Three children will each fold the same number of papers. How many papers will each child fold?

a. 63
b. 59
c. 56
d. 55

A

B

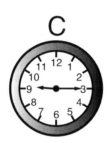

C

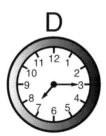

D

38. Which of the above clocks show a time between 7:00 and 8:00?

    a. clock **A** only
    b. clock **B** and clock **C**
    c. clock **A** and clock **D**
    d. clock **D** only

39. A quadrilateral with four sides of equal length and four right angles is called a

    a. rhombus.
    b. trapezoid.
    c. pentagon.
    d. square.

40. Morgan has five square-shaped pieces of paper. He cut each square in half diagonally. When added together, how many sides did all of these new shapes have?

    a. 40
    b. 36
    c. 30
    d. 25

    T21   **PLEASE GO ON TO THE NEXT PAGE.**

Favorite Sport	
Soccer	ҬҲҬ ҬҲҬ ǀǀ
Baseball	ҬҲҬ ǀǀǀǀ
Hockey	ǀǀǀǀ
Football	ҬҲҬ ҬҲҬ
Auto Racing	ǀǀǀ
Basketball	ҬҲҬ ҬҲҬ
Tennis	ǀǀ

41. According to the tally chart, which sport did the third-grade students choose the LEAST?

    a. tennis
    b. hockey
    c. football
    d. auto racing

42. How many students chose hockey as their favorite sport?

    a. three
    b. four
    c. nine
    d. twelve

T22   **PLEASE GO ON TO THE NEXT PAGE.**

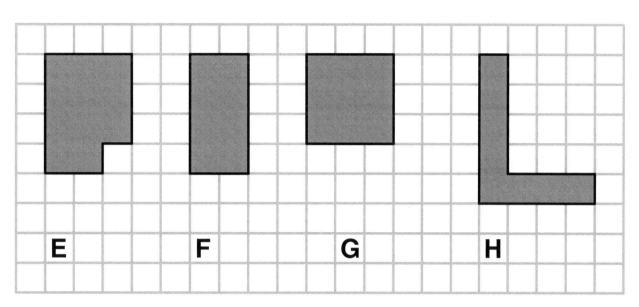

E   F   G   H

☐ ↕ = 1 inch

43. Which of the figures shown in the above diagram have the SAME perimeter?

a. figures **F** and **G**
b. figures **E** and **H**
c. figures **G** and **H**
d. figures **F** and **H**

T23

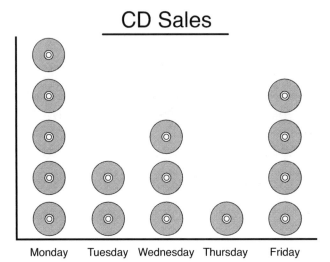

CD Sales

Day of the Week

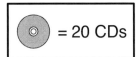 = 20 CDs

44. Last week, Busy Bee Records kept track of their CD sales. This data is shown in the above pictograph. Create a bar graph that would show this data.

T24

PLEASE STOP! YOU HAVE
REACHED THE END OF PART TWO.

STOP!

Use this page to do calculations or for additional space in answering the constructed-response problems.

Use this page to do calculations or for additional space in answering the constructed-response problems.

Use this page to do calculations or for additional space in answering the constructed-response problems.

Use this page to do calculations or for additional space in answering the constructed-response problems.

Pretest Answer Grid
Multiple-Choice Problems

Part 1

1 ⓐ ⓑ ⓒ ⓓ
2 ⓐ ⓑ ⓒ ⓓ
3 ⓐ ⓑ ⓒ ⓓ
4 ⓐ ⓑ ⓒ ⓓ
5 ⓐ ⓑ ⓒ ⓓ
6 ⓐ ⓑ ⓒ ⓓ
7 ⓐ ⓑ ⓒ ⓓ
8 ⓐ ⓑ ⓒ ⓓ
9 ⓐ ⓑ ⓒ ⓓ
10 ⓐ ⓑ ⓒ ⓓ
11 ⓐ ⓑ ⓒ ⓓ

12 ⓐ ⓑ ⓒ ⓓ
13 ⓐ ⓑ ⓒ ⓓ
14 ⓐ ⓑ ⓒ ⓓ
15 ⓐ ⓑ ⓒ ⓓ
16 ⓐ ⓑ ⓒ ⓓ
17 ⓐ ⓑ ⓒ ⓓ
18 ⓐ ⓑ ⓒ ⓓ
19 ⓐ ⓑ ⓒ ⓓ
20 ⓐ ⓑ ⓒ ⓓ
21 ⓐ ⓑ ⓒ ⓓ

Part 2

23 ⓐ ⓑ ⓒ ⓓ
24 ⓐ ⓑ ⓒ ⓓ
25 ⓐ ⓑ ⓒ ⓓ
26 ⓐ ⓑ ⓒ ⓓ
27 ⓐ ⓑ ⓒ ⓓ
28 ⓐ ⓑ ⓒ ⓓ
29 ⓐ ⓑ ⓒ ⓓ
30 ⓐ ⓑ ⓒ ⓓ
31 ⓐ ⓑ ⓒ ⓓ
32 ⓐ ⓑ ⓒ ⓓ
33 ⓐ ⓑ ⓒ ⓓ

34 ⓐ ⓑ ⓒ ⓓ
35 ⓐ ⓑ ⓒ ⓓ
36 ⓐ ⓑ ⓒ ⓓ
37 ⓐ ⓑ ⓒ ⓓ
38 ⓐ ⓑ ⓒ ⓓ
39 ⓐ ⓑ ⓒ ⓓ
40 ⓐ ⓑ ⓒ ⓓ
41 ⓐ ⓑ ⓒ ⓓ
42 ⓐ ⓑ ⓒ ⓓ
43 ⓐ ⓑ ⓒ ⓓ

Problems 22 and 44 are constructed-response problems. Make sure to clearly write your solutions to these problems directly in the practice test pages.

This part of the test contains twenty-one multiple-choice problems and one constructed-response problem. Be sure to show all your work when solving the constructed-response problem. Any calculations may be written directly on the pages in this section or in the additional work space on pages T55 through T58. You may also use this additional work space if you need more room to write your answer to the constructed-response problem. Your answer to this problem must be clearly labeled regardless of where it appears in the practice test.

If you cannot solve a problem, go on to the next one. If you have time, you may go back and try to solve any problems that you skipped *in this section only*.

You have **seventy-five minutes** to complete this part of the test.

Calculators ARE NOT allowed for this part of the test!

PLEASE GO ON TO THE NEXT PAGE.

1. The number 4,837 can be grouped as

   a. three thousands, three hundreds, eight tens, and seven ones.
   b. four thousands, eight hundreds, three tens, and seven ones.
   c. four thousands, seven hundreds, four tens, and seven ones.
   d. three thousands, eight hundreds, three tens, and seventeen ones.

800 + 90 + 5

3. How would the above number be written in standard form?

   a. 598
   b. 958
   c. 985
   d. 895

O ■ O ■ □ O ■ □ ■ O

2. Which of the following would MOST LIKELY come next in order to continue the pattern shown above?

   a.

   b.

   c.

   d.

T32   PLEASE GO ON TO THE NEXT PAGE.

A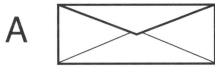

10 envelopes

C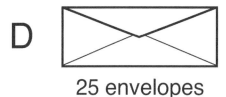

20 envelopes

B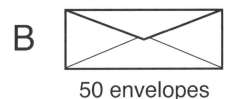

50 envelopes

D

25 envelopes

4.   Monica needs exactly 60 envelopes to mail 60 letters. Envelopes could be purchased in boxes with each box containing the number of envelopes shown in the above diagram. If Monica were to buy three boxes of envelopes, which of the following would result in her buying EXACTLY 60 envelopes?

a. three of box D
b. two of box A and one of box B
c. three of box C
d. one of box A, one of box B, and one of box C

$1.30 $1.65, $2.00, $2.35, _____

5.   What amount would come next in the pattern shown above?

a. $2.50
b. $2.70
c. $3.05
d. $2.85

6.   Steven has 950 baseball cards. He gave 460 of these cards to his younger brother. How many baseball cards does Steven now have?

a. 510
b. 490
c. 450
d. 440

T33   PLEASE GO ON TO THE NEXT PAGE.

7. Which of the following number sentences can be used to find the number of geese in the above diagram?

   a. 4 x 6 =
   b. 3 x 7 =
   c. 5 x 8 =
   d. 2 x 10 =

125, 100, 75, 50 ?

8. Which of the following would be the next number in the pattern shown above?

   a. 35
   b. 50
   c. 75
   d. 25

9. If the nine in the number 973 were replaced by a five, the number

   a. would increase by 400.
   b. would decrease by 400.
   c. would increase by 40.
   d. would decrease by 40.

10. A piece of wood is 42 inches long. It is

    a. more than one yard long.
    b. less than one yard long.
    c. equal to one yard long.
    d. equal to four feet long.

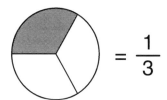 $= \dfrac{1}{3}$

13. Which of the following fractional parts of the circle is equal to one-third?

11. A bus traveled 415 miles on Thursday and 573 miles on Friday. Altogether, how many miles did the bus travel in these two days?

    a. 927
    b. 988
    c. 841
    d. 962

a.  $= \dfrac{2}{6}$

b. $= \dfrac{2}{8}$

12. Manny has to subtract 219 from 909. Which of the following would be BEST for Manny to use to ESTIMATE the difference?

    a. 900 - 200
    b. 800 - 200
    c. 900 - 300
    d. 900 - 400

c. $= \dfrac{1}{6}$

d. $= \dfrac{3}{8}$

T35

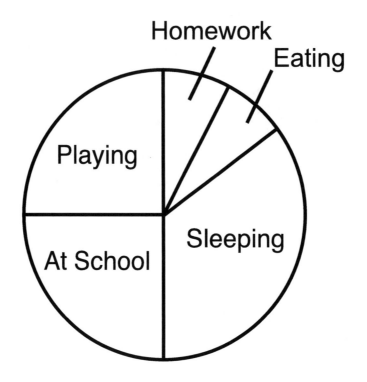

ADAM'S DAY

14. The above graph shows what Adam did yesterday. Adam spent the greatest amount of time

a. doing homework.
b. playing.
c. at school.
d. sleeping.

T36

15. Last Saturday, Yuri went jogging in the park. Including Yuri, there were only four joggers. This Saturday, there are three times as many joggers in the park than there were last Saturday. Which of the following diagrams BEST shows the number of joggers in the park this Saturday?

a.

c.

b.

d.

T37 PLEASE GO ON TO THE NEXT PAGE.

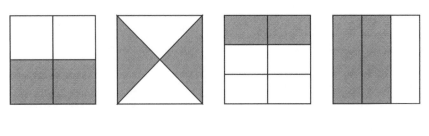

1 **2** **3** **4**

16. In which two figures does the shaded part show the SAME fraction?

    a. figures 3 and 4
    b. figures 2 and 4
    c. figures 1 and 3
    d. figures 1 and 2

Number of CDs	2	3	4	5	6	7
Cost	$14.00	$21.00	$28.00	$35.00	$42.00	$49.00

17. Hannah's favorite store in the mall is having a sale on CDs. If the pattern in the chart continues, how much will she have to pay for eight CDs?

    a. $63.00
    b. $52.00
    c. $56.00
    d. $70.00

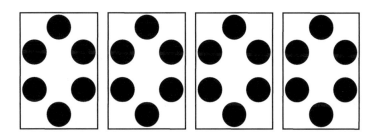

18. Jake found the total number of dots in the above diagram by saying
    "6 + 6 + 6 + 6 = 24." Which of the following expressions can also be used to
    solve this problem?

    a. 16 + 4
    b. 6 x 4
    c. 2 x 20
    d. (6 - 4) x 6

19. Jamie is planting a flower bed like the one shown above. If Jamie plants 16
    roses in each of the four rows of her flower bed, how many roses will she have
    planted in all?

    a. 72 roses
    b. 64 roses
    c. 48 roses
    d. 56 roses

 PLEASE GO ON TO THE NEXT PAGE.

The graph below shows how many different kinds of pets were sold at the local pet store this past weekend.

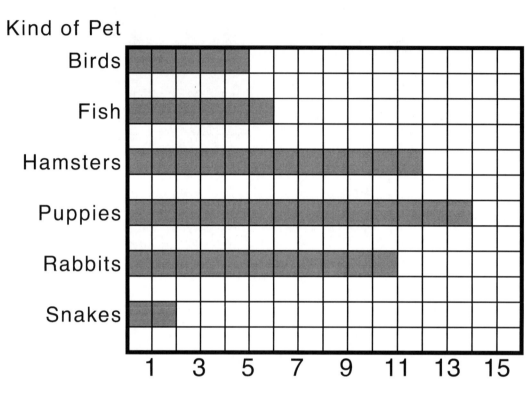

20. According to the graph, how many pets were sold altogether?

    a. 42
    b. 46
    c. 50
    d. 54

PLEASE GO ON TO THE NEXT PAGE.

21. Harper Elementary School held a fundraiser. The first grade raised a total of $275.00. The second grade raised ninety dollars less than the first grade. The third grade raised a total of $340.00. The fourth grade raised sixty-five dollars more than the third grade. Which of the following tables correctly shows the amount of money each grade raised?

a.

Grade	Money Raised
1	$275.00
2	$185.00
3	$340.00
4	$405.00

c.

Grade	Money Raised
1	$185.00
2	$275.00
3	$340.00
4	$405.00

b.

Grade	Money Raised
1	$275.00
2	$185.00
3	$405.00
4	$340.00

d.

Grade	Money Raised
1	$185.00
2	$275.00
3	$405.00
4	$340.00

 PLEASE GO ON TO THE NEXT PAGE.

a

b

c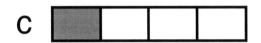

d

e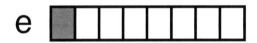

Match each picture shown above to the fraction that the shaded part of each picture represents. Each picture will be used only once.

22a.   one-half   _____

22b.   one-third   _____

22c.   one-fourth   _____

22e.   one-sixth   _____

22e.   one-eighth   _____

T42

PLEASE STOP! YOU HAVE REACHED THE END OF PART ONE. STOP!

This part of the test contains twenty-one multiple-choice problems and one constructed-response problem. Be sure to show all your work when solving the constructed-response problem. Any calculations may be written directly on the pages in this section or in the additional work space on pages T55 through T58. You may also use this additional work space if you need more room to write your answer to the constructed-response problem. Your answer to this problem must be clearly labeled regardless of where it appears in the practice test.

If you cannot solve a problem, go on to the next one. If you have time, you may go back and try to solve any problems that you skipped *in this section only*.

If you complete Part Two of the test, you CANNOT return to any previous parts to work on problems you have either skipped over or failed to complete.

You have **seventy-five minutes** to complete this part of the test.

Calculators ARE NOT allowed for this part of the test!

Number of Fish Caught on Fishing Trip

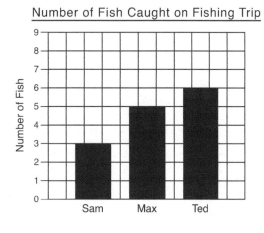

23. Which of the following bar graphs BEST represents the information shown in the above pictograph?

a.

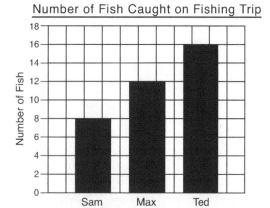

c.

b.

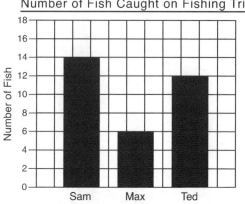

d.

24. Brian found the coins shown above on the floor of his mother's car. Which of the following would be the total value of these coins?

    a. $0.77
    b. $0.97
    c. $0.87
    d. $0.67

(8 + 1) + 5 = 8 + (? + 5)

25. Which number makes the above number sentence TRUE?

    a. 1
    b. 5
    c. 6
    d. 9

26. Sandy was given the following numbers to add: 3, 8, 9, 2, 1, and 7. Sandy added (3 + 7), (9 + 1), and (8 + 2). Which properties of addition did Sandy use to find the sum of these numbers?

    a. distributive and identity properties
    b. associative and commutative properties
    c. commutative and inverse properties
    d. distributive and associative properties

(9 x 7) - 5 = ___ - 5

27. Which of the following numbers would replace the blank line in order to make the above number sentence TRUE?

    a. 16
    b. 63
    c. 58
    d. 68

T45 PLEASE GO ON TO THE NEXT PAGE.

28. Which of the following thermometers shows a temperature of 46°?

a.   b.   c.   d.

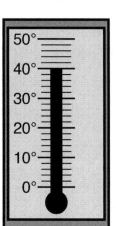  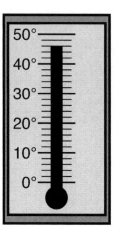 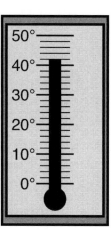

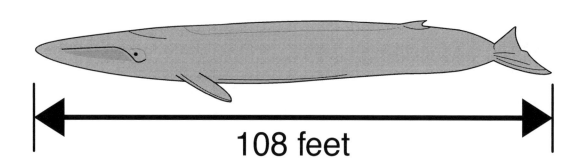

108 feet

29. The longest blue whale ever recorded measured 108 feet. How many yards is 108 feet?

a. 324 yards
b. 9 yards
c. 36 yards
d. 3 yards

T46   **PLEASE GO ON TO THE NEXT PAGE.**

Trout Caught Daily

Mon.	🐟 🐟
Tues.	🐟 🐟 🐟 🐟 🐟
Wed.	🐟 🐟 🐟 🐟 🐟 🐟
Thurs.	🐟 🐟 🐟 🐟 🐟
Fri.	🐟 🐟 🐟

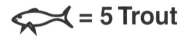 = 5 Trout

30. Based on the information in the pictograph shown above, which of the following statements is NOT true?

   a. The most trout were caught on Wednesday.
   b. Less than 12 trout were caught on Friday.
   c. The same number of trout were caught on Tuesday and Thursday.
   d. Less than 12 trout were caught on Monday.

T47   PLEASE GO ON TO THE NEXT PAGE.

31. Twenty third graders were asked which sports they play after school. Seven third graders play only soccer, five play only basketball, and four play only hockey. In addition, three play soccer and basketball and one plays soccer and hockey. Which of the following Venn diagrams BEST shows this information?

a.

Sports Played by Third Graders

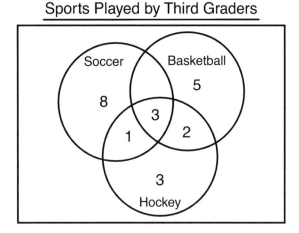

c.

Sports Played by Third Graders

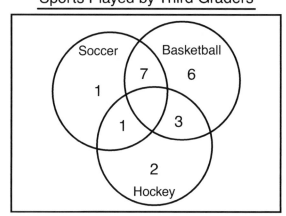

b.

Sports Played by Third Graders

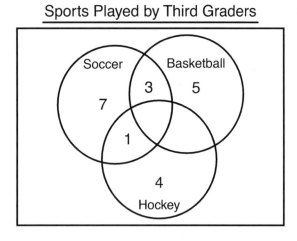

d.

Sports Played by Third Graders

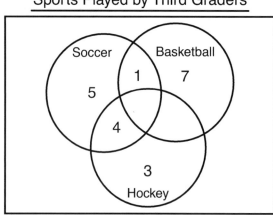

T48 PLEASE GO ON TO THE NEXT PAGE.

figure 1

figure 2

figure 3

figure 4

32. Which figure shown above has the LEAST number of sides?

   a. figure 4
   b. figure 3
   c. figure 2
   d. figure 1

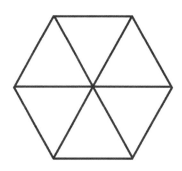

33. Which shape below CANNOT be made by tracing the lines in the hexagon shown above?

a.

b.

c.

d.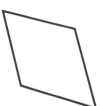

T49 PLEASE GO ON TO THE NEXT PAGE.

34. If Yolanda looked at the bottom of the orange juice carton shown above, which of the following shapes would she MOST LIKELY see?

a.

b.

c.

d.

35. The points A, B, C, D, E, and F are connected by line segments. Point F is connected to point A by one of these segments. What kind of figure will be formed by the connection of these points with line segments?

a. a triangle
b. a square
c. a pentagon
d. a hexagon

36. Donna works at her job five days a week from 8:00 a.m. to 4:30 p.m. Yesterday, she started working thirty minutes earlier than usual. At which of the following times did Donna start working yesterday?

a. 7:00 a.m.
b. 7:30 a.m.
c. 8:30 a.m.
d. 7:15 a.m.

37. Trina is cooking rice on her stove. The instructions say to cook the rice for 45 minutes. If the rice starts cooking at 4:45, at which of the following times should the rice be done?

a. 5:15
b. 5:30
c. 5:45
d. 6:00

T50   PLEASE GO ON TO THE NEXT PAGE.

38. Dina bought an orange that cost 59 cents. She paid for it with a one-dollar bill. Which of the following groups of coins shows the correct amount of change that Dina should have received?

a.

b.

c.

d.

39. Ronna has 307 baseball cards. Leslie has 788 cards, and Marci has 911 cards. Which of the following would give the BEST ESTIMATE of the total number of cards Ronna, Leslie, and Marci have altogether?

   a. 400 + 800 + 700
   b. 500 + 600 + 700
   c. 300 + 800 + 900
   d. 200 + 800 + 800

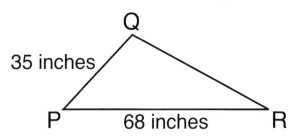

40. The perimeter of triangle PQR shown above is 157 inches. What is the length of side QR?

   a. 122 inches
   b. 68 inches
   c. 89 inches
   d. 54 inches

T51 PLEASE GO ON TO THE NEXT PAGE.

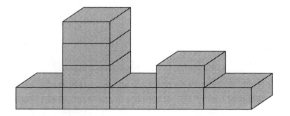

1 ▱ = 5 pounds

41. How many more bricks have to be added to the above diagram in order to make the stack of bricks equal 50 pounds?

   a. 5 bricks
   b. 1 brick
   c. 2 bricks
   d. 10 bricks

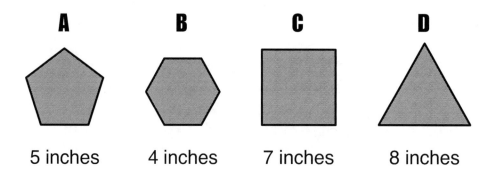

A	B	C	D
5 inches	4 inches	7 inches	8 inches

42. Each of the figures shown in the above diagram is a regular polygon. The length of one of the sides of each figure is also shown. Which of these figures has the LARGEST perimeter?

   a. figure **A**
   b. figure **B**
   c. figure **C**
   d. figure **D**

Cats Treated at Lakewood Animal Hospital

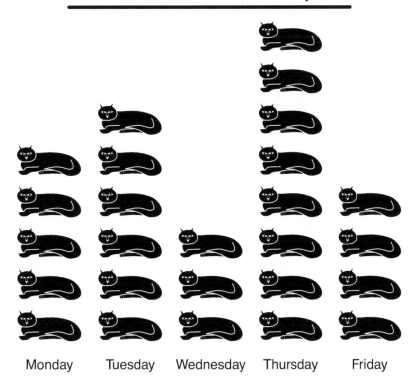

Monday   Tuesday   Wednesday   Thursday   Friday

Day of the Week

1 🐈 = 3 cats

The above pictograph shows the number of cats treated at Lakewood Animal Hospital last week.

43.   On which day were the GREATEST number of cats treated?

a. Friday
b. Monday
c. Thursday
d. Tuesday

T53   PLEASE GO ON TO THE NEXT PAGE.

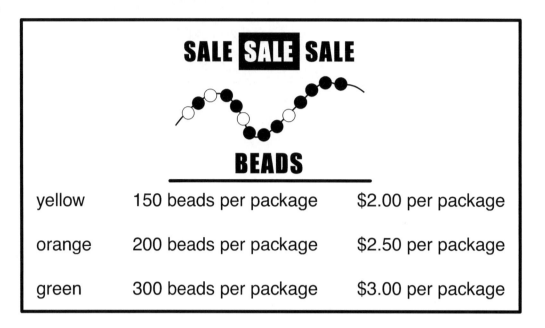

SALE **SALE** SALE

BEADS

yellow	150 beads per package	$2.00 per package
orange	200 beads per package	$2.50 per package
green	300 beads per package	$3.00 per package

Tracie wants to make some necklaces for a few of her friends. She will buy beads that are on sale as advertised in the above sign, and will buy the beads based on the following information:

- Tracie will buy at least one package of each color bead.
- Tracie will buy at least twelve packages of beads.
- Tracie will buy EXACTLY 3,000 beads.
- Tracie will spend $35.00 or less on these beads.

44. Fill in the chart below to correctly reflect the above information.

Bead Color	Packages Bought	Number of Beads	Amount Spent
yellow			
orange			
green			
Totals			

PLEASE STOP! YOU HAVE
REACHED THE END OF PART TWO.

STOP!

Use this page to do calculations or for additional space in answering the constructed-response problems.

Use this page to do calculations or for additional space in answering the constructed-response problems.

Use this page to do calculations or for additional space in answering the constructed-response problems.

Additional Work Space

Use this page to do calculations or for additional space in answering the constructed-response problems.

Posttest Answer Grid
Multiple-Choice Problems

Part 1

1 (a) (b) (c) (d)
2 (a) (b) (c) (d)
3 (a) (b) (c) (d)
4 (a) (b) (c) (d)
5 (a) (b) (c) (d)
6 (a) (b) (c) (d)
7 (a) (b) (c) (d)
8 (a) (b) (c) (d)
9 (a) (b) (c) (d)
10 (a) (b) (c) (d)
11 (a) (b) (c) (d)

12 (a) (b) (c) (d)
13 (a) (b) (c) (d)
14 (a) (b) (c) (d)
15 (a) (b) (c) (d)
16 (a) (b) (c) (d)
17 (a) (b) (c) (d)
18 (a) (b) (c) (d)
19 (a) (b) (c) (d)
20 (a) (b) (c) (d)
21 (a) (b) (c) (d)

Part 2

23 (a) (b) (c) (d)
24 (a) (b) (c) (d)
25 (a) (b) (c) (d)
26 (a) (b) (c) (d)
27 (a) (b) (c) (d)
28 (a) (b) (c) (d)
29 (a) (b) (c) (d)
30 (a) (b) (c) (d)
31 (a) (b) (c) (d)
32 (a) (b) (c) (d)
33 (a) (b) (c) (d)

34 (a) (b) (c) (d)
35 (a) (b) (c) (d)
36 (a) (b) (c) (d)
37 (a) (b) (c) (d)
38 (a) (b) (c) (d)
39 (a) (b) (c) (d)
40 (a) (b) (c) (d)
41 (a) (b) (c) (d)
42 (a) (b) (c) (d)
43 (a) (b) (c) (d)

Problems 22 and 44 are constructed-response problems. Make sure to clearly write your solutions to these problems directly in the practice test pages.

Made in the USA
Middletown, DE
14 January 2020

83205223R00121